Death of the Snake Oil Salesman

Book One: Opening the Deal

Bernard J. Jones

PARTRIDGE

A Penguin Random House Company

To order additional copies of this book, contact
Toll Free 800 101 2657 (Singapore)
Toll Free 1 800 81 7340 (Malaysia)
orders.singapore@partridgepublishing.com

www.partridgepublishing.com/singapore

Death of the Snake Oil Salesman

The species known as the Snake Oil Salesman, sadly, is in rapid decline, almost dead in modern business. The swindler who could sell sand to Arabs, ice to the Eskimos and coal to Newcastle is a thing of the past. There were some real characters out there (and still are), but customers are smarter now. They want the product to work and produce results. Value for money—not some silver-tongued shyster who's full of false promises.

The end of an era, I say, wiping a tear from my eye, as I was one of them. I bid them farewell, and all the best. And while it was originally a male domain, there are now a lot of Snake Oil Saleswomen as well.

They don't mean to offend anyone. They just see selling as an easy way of making money. Tragically, this short-term view usually equates to a short-lived career. These days, everyone sees through the rogue like a pane of glass. Really quickly. The Snake Oil Salesman / woman is a thing of the past. Dead. Long live the Sales Partner!

In this practical, two-part book of proven selling techniques I show the two stages of winning business. You work as partners with your clients to:

1. Open the deal, and
2. Close the deal

Take your prospects and customers through the steps in a genuine way. Look at selling as a partnership where you address each party's interests. It's all about how you think and behave.

This book deals with Stage One—Opening the Deal. Enjoy the ride. Sorry, the read. And bid farewell to that odious Product-Pushing Snake Oil Salesman once and for all.

BERNARD J. JONES

Definition of a Snake Oil Salesman

"Snake Oil Salesman" is an American term for a peddler of medicinal remedies with no therapeutic value other than the psychosomatic. Someone who recommends a product that will make him or her money, without caring whether it has any benefit to the customer.

A person of dubious trust. A purveyor of doubtful products. A person who ingratiates the buyer, sells things of no value, then disappears. A shyster. Cares only for himself or herself.

DEDICATION

For my beautiful family, Kath, Caleb, Victoria.

ACKNOWLEDGEMENTS

Thank you to all of our clients, for trusting us to train your people. Particularly Gavin Mortlock, our first client 12 years ago, and who is still our client today. And Cynthia Ng, who really knocked us into shape as a training business.

All of the people I have met in my professional (some may well laugh) life who have shaped my career and who possibly feature in this story. Especially my great friend Tom Karnasuta, who has met more sales people than anyone I know. He taught me how to sell. And Wayne Shah, the brilliant cash flow / business process analyst who knew more about most clients' business than they themselves knew.

My editors and advisors, Michael McKinnon, Scott Dixon and Carol Campbell, who taught me how to write at the age of 50. My mate Stuey Diamond, for making me think about monetising our knowledge.

My illustrator, friend and erstwhile colleague, Peter Groenewoud, the original partnership sales guy. Thanks for the excellent sketches and for our superb memories of working on "the big deal".

My bemused colleagues at Chase in the Singapore '90s—Brian Moran, Nick Franck, Jimmy Yap, Kate Jackson, Mark Powell, Kevan Albrighton, Mike Whitehead, Hiten Joshi and Joe Stark— who patiently coached me to become a salesman while probably wishing they'd never met me.

My great mates John Crouch and Rod Wood, who dubbed me the Snake Oil Salesman back in 1990. And Steve Douglas, Jason Reed Wagner and Charles Hamilton Ferguson, the entrepreneurs.

Mostly my wife Kathryn Mary McMahon, who has inspired me to run a business and has always believed in my ability to string together a good book. Let's hope it lives up to those expectations.

Let's face it. If you can't sell a book on selling, you shouldn't waste your time writing it in the first place!

The Value-Adding Team

INTRODUCTION

John doesn't sell. He is an IT professional, a geek. He thinks sales people are "like, weird".

I asked him, "Do you sell in your job, John?"

He laughed at me disdainfully. "Of course not, I'd never do that, um, sell, like, I, well I just couldn't do that, that's like, all those cowboy insurance guys and stuff."

I persisted.

"So how did you get your job, John? Did someone see you walking along and said, 'Hey, John, you look like an IT kinda guy. We've got a mainframe with loads of Legacy applications we're trying to migrate. We've got a great job for you. You can start Monday! Congratulations, welcome to the team! By the way John, how much money do you want?' Is that how you got your job, John?"

John was startled by this provocative question: "No, of course not."

"Well, what happened? How did you get your job?"

"I applied for it, of course."

"How?"

Looking like a witness struggling in the dock. "Well, I um, ah, saw a job advertisement on the internet and thought I'd apply."

"Why?"

Confused. "Well, why not? I wasn't happy where I was and wasn't making enough money."

"Oh, so you had needs that were not being met?"

"Well, yes, I suppose so, but I've never thought about it like that before."

"Right, and what about your prospective employer. What were they looking for?"

"Oh well, all of my skills, really. They needed someone holding senior roles both in applications management and infrastructure management, across both corporate and consumer banking."

I had *no* idea what he was talking about.

"OK, so they had needs that were not being met, too?"

"Yes, if you put it like that. They did."

"So you applied for the job, matching your skills and experience to their needs. Is that what happened, John?"

Impatient now. "Yes, I did. Of course I did. I looked at every criterion they had and wrote something about what I'd done in this field. It's logical. What's the big deal?"

Sensing I'm losing my interviewee. "Two more questions please, John—one, did you tell them how well you did these things?"

Annoyed by now, as I was distracting him from developing PowerPoint slides: "Yes, I did, as a matter of fact. I gave an example for each point. What's your other question?"

"Why did you do that?"

Looking at me as if I was an imbecile. "Because I wanted to convince them I was the best person for the job, of course!"

"Thank you, Your Honour. No further witnesses. I rest my case. Everybody sells."

John, IT geek

We all sell

Most people do not see themselves as salespeople. This is someone else's job, thankfully not their own. Some people seem to be "born salespeople". They're the smooth talkers, the easygoing types who mix it with everyone. These people are mistrusted the most.

Why? They bend too much—everything's doable, too unstructured, too easy. "No worries! Of course we can do that. We are the best." Boy, does that bring back memories!

But they are the obvious salespeople. We all sell in our own way. We may, for example, drive hard on an issue to get it resolved. Or we may set very high standards for our team members, so quality is assured. On the other hand, we may set and stick to agendas and document details in order to control a project.

Selling is about getting things done—meeting your needs and others' needs at the same time. It takes two to tango. We all do it. We all have our good sides and bad. And you are probably better at it than you've ever given yourself credit for.

And it's helpful to put a structure to it. I call it IMPACT Selling. This spells the Death of the Product-Pusher—the Snake Oil Salesman.

CHAPTER 1

The Snake Oil Salesman

Pushy, cocky, aggressive, egotistical, arrogant, manipulative, money-hungry . . .

Looking back, these are the words my customers and colleagues would have used to describe me during my first 12 months in sales. I worked for a bank and we had a great product. It was new and saved customers tons of money. They loved the product because it made them look good. So, my job was all about selling the product. And the more I sold, the more money I made. It was as simple as that. What a great job!

The customers, the companies we sold to? Who were they? What did they do? What business were they in? I didn't know and didn't care. It didn't matter to me.

I didn't *need* to know anything about them—that was someone else's job. All I had to do was make an appointment, turn up, and one of my colleagues would talk about the product. I got the commission. I was on easy street—the product sold itself.

If there was a problem with the product after we sold it, that wasn't *my* concern. I wouldn't have to deal with the issue or speak to the customer again. That's what Customer Service was for! I just eased my way out of the train wreck and moved on to the next prospect. What a baptism into the world of selling.

Looking back, I'm surprised anyone bought anything from me. Many of my colleagues couldn't stand me. But I didn't care—I was in *Sales*. I was putting *my* job on the line.

If I didn't sell, I would get fired—not like them in *their* cushy jobs. And if Sales didn't bring in the money, they wouldn't have a job anyway. I used to remind them of that whenever they had the temerity to challenge my Snake Oil Salesman approach.

What's the first term that springs to mind when you hear the word "salesman"? *Talkative, slippery, commission-driven, greedy, untrustworthy, coercive, tricky . . .*

This was me. The *"ultimate Snake Oil Salesman"* was how one of my colleagues described me.

And, over the past 15 years, I have asked this question to more than 10,000 businesspeople in all parts of the world. "What's the first word you think of when you hear "salesman?" And that is what they say. *Dishonest, unscrupulous, a shyster, a schmoozer, Sir Lunchalot . . . . the list goes on.* Even salespeople use these words to describe others in their own profession!

Why?

Because most salespeople talk too much. They don't listen. And the problem is that you just can't understand someone else's needs when you're talking.

As the Snake Oil Salesman, it's all about me. It's all about what *I* want. And what I want is to exceed my target so I get the bonus, the commission, the big fat paycheque—the money. I can make more money in this job than I can in *any* other job.

I have my sales target, my product and my prospect. And I think the best way to get the prospect to buy is to tell them how great the product is. I have convinced myself of the amazing features of this product and just want to tell everyone about it (even if I don't believe it).

The Snake Oil Salesman in natural pose

Spray & Pray—The Shotgun Approach

I keep talking even if the other person is telling me they're not interested. That's just a challenge that can be overcome with persistence and more information and pressure.

As the year progresses and my sales performance begins to lag behind target, I become more desperate to sell. I ramp up my calling program so I can tell more people about the great product I have.

There is a science behind this sales approach. It's called Spray & Pray. And there is no doubt it works, sometimes. If you spray enough out there, some of it will stick.

I *will* get lucky and someone *will* be interested enough to buy from me. Or maybe they will buy just to get rid of me. Spray & Pray is only slightly more reliable than buying a lottery ticket. It's a whisker away from spam.

It's also called the Shotgun Approach. Look inside a shotgun cartridge. There are hundreds of tiny metal balls. When you pull a shotgun trigger a swarm of these pellets is sprayed at the target. A shotgun is a favorite tool of hunters, because there is more chance of hitting the moving target.

See, finally got a couple. I told you the shotgun approach works!
The Shot-Gun Approach: Spray & Pray

And that explains the mentality of many salespeople.

The moving target is the prospect, trying to get away from the Snake Oil Salesman. They may not be physically moving, but they are mentally wriggling around throwing up all kinds of reasons why they're not interested. These are called *objections*.

But the salesman just keeps spraying, because just maybe one of these pellets will stick.

"Insanity is doing the same thing, over and over again, but expecting different results." (Albert Einstein)

You almost have to admire these salespeople's persistence. They experience the stresses of opportunity, hope, anxiety, rejection, outright failure and occasional success every day—and this is the life they love, the only life they know.

But I also feel sorry for these poor bastards because so much effort is wasted. There is a better way!

Creating value

What do the most successful salespeople do? They create value. They have some structure to engage their prospects and customers. They work in partnership to help their customer improve their business.

There are many different models and approaches but the main ingredients are:

- Studying the market's need for their products, classifying their potential customer base, identifying specific customers, researching them, meeting them and finding out about their business.
- Discussing what is important to the customer, their goals, finding out about the challenges to be faced and understanding the processes that contribute to those challenges.
- Objectively quantifying the scope of the various challenges and working out which are the most important to fix.
- Discussing solutions the client has tried before and their ideas on what they are looking for *now.*
- Designing or finding a product or service that addresses the issue and helps make the client's life easier—and is profitable for the seller.
- Presenting the solution, and agreeing the terms and implementation timeframe.
- Making sure it works to the customer's approval and following up to check for ongoing satisfaction.
- Looking for additional ways of building the relationship.

Successful salespeople don't do all the talking. They ask the customer to talk about themselves and what *they* are interested in. Then they try to find ways to help the customer address their interests.

Key points

- People open up when you focus on what is interesting to them, not to you. You have two ears and one mouth— use them in proportion.
- If you talk about product features without knowing if customers are interested, they close down. And if you persist, you create a negative experience the customer will not want to repeat. They will tell people about the experience and your name will be mud. *"If you ever get a call from this guy, just tell him you are too busy. He's a Snake Oil Salesman!"*
- People are motivated by their own interests, not yours. Your role in sales is to understand your clients' interests and make them your own. Put yourself in the customer's shoes and wear them around for a while until you feel the pain and get the blisters.
- You will soon know where the pain is and how much it hurts. You will then be in a good position to work together to find or build the solution they need. Then you can deliver the extras they don't expect.

**The Snake Oil Salesman's view
"Who cares about what other
people want? My job is to
sell, sell, sell. If I tell enough
people about my product,
some idiot will buy. Selling's
a numbers game—nothing
more! Now, where are we
going for lunch, and who's
paying?"**

CHAPTER 2

Self-belief

A great friend of mine was reviewing this book. He is a top dog at a big bank, and after reading it said to me:

"You've got to put something in about belief in your product. If you don't believe in what you're selling, you may as well do something else."

I agree with this and will add something more. Believe in yourself, your unique ability to do whatever you want.

Everyone is different, with different interests and goals. Some want to be rich, some want to be famous, some want to just get the job done. Others want to improve things, make a difference in others' lives, help the needy or dazzle the world with brilliance. Whatever your world is, you will surprise yourself at what you can achieve, if you do *one* thing.

Try something new.

Trying something new implies rejecting fear of failure. In itself, this action is a success. Whether you do it well or poorly, if it works or doesn't work, doesn't matter. The act of *doing* it contributes another success to your Pool of Life Experiences.

Another triumph over self-doubt. The more instances you have of conquering fear of failure, the more confidence you have in your ability to overcome the next kick in the teeth.

> **"The oldest and strongest emotion of mankind**
> **is fear, and the oldest and strongest kind of fear**
> **is fear of the unknown." (H. P. Lovecraft)**

We draw upon this pool with every challenge in life. The more new things you try, the more confident you become.

Winning the deal feeds confidence and gives you a positive view of the future. More importantly, when you lose the deal, self-belief picks you up by your shirt and drives your determination to win the next one.

"We lost the Concorde deal."

"Bummer. After all that work we put in. There goes the holiday in California. OK, let's get on with Oriental Bank. What do we have to do to win that?"

Case Study 1: The Fruit Salesman

I spoke briefly to the guy in the wine shop today. He was busy unpacking a carton of bottles and shoving them on a shelf. Not very caringly, I thought. I was the only customer in the shop but he ignored me, busily scooping up cardboard scraps and string.

"Any decent specials from New Zealand?" I asked, smiling, friendly.

"I don't know any wines. I just work here."

That's odd, I thought. It *is* a wine shop. Undeterred, I selected a couple of sauvignon blancs and he was waiting for me at the cash register. He smiled as he took the bottles and put them in the bag. He rang up the amount and I handed him the cash.

"My last day today," he announced, looking happy. "This job not a good fit."

"Oh," I said, "what are you going to do?"

"Sales."

"Great . . . what will you be selling?"

"I don't know. Fruit, or something."

I was in a hurry so I didn't take it any further. I shook his hand, wished him luck and left the shop. Sitting back in my office I thought this extraordinary. A man in his late forties resigns from his job and does not know what he is going to be doing the next day, except "sales".

In hindsight, maybe he was leaving the job because he had no interest in wine. Fair enough. But he didn't sound *that* interested in fruit either. Maybe he was, but he didn't look too excited about it.

He had no passion, no drive and I felt for the guy—who would hire him? Would I want to pick him up and coach him and try to change the attitude? Nope, I haven't got time. Even if I did, he would probably quit in three months or get fired. Unless he was in the field he loved, his passion. If you believe in what you are doing and love it, you *will* be able to sell it. And when you get knocked back and someone else gets the deal, you keep going.

And maybe that's the difference between an ordinary salesperson and a successful one. To some people it's just a job "selling fruit or something". It's a struggle, an existence full of disappointments, a means to an end. For others it's *living the dream*. The struggle is the best part, the defining test.

> ***"Failure is the bitter pill that makes victory***
> ***the sweetest taste of all" (Anon)***

Belief in your ability to overcome setbacks is the secret of all triumphs.

Some compelling questions

1. Must I believe in my product?

    Answer: If you don't, why are you wasting your life? Do something else.

2. How do I believe in myself?

    Answer: Try something new. Don't judge success by the outcome, judge it by the size of the risk you overcame to try it. It shows you can do anything. When you know that, you believe in yourself.

3. How do I become more confident?

Answer: It's called Rational Thinking, which drives confidence. If you see every setback as a disaster, you are on the road to doom. You cannot change the past, so don't spend one second regretting it. Learn to think rationally about it. So we lost the big deal. Did we die? No. Did we lose everything we own? No. Did someone get sick? No. OK—what's the worst thing that could possibly happen? We can't afford to go to California for the holiday. Who knows, maybe we could have got mugged if we went there. Maybe we didn't get this deal for a reason.

Note: Thoughts & Feelings by McKay and Davis gives an in-depth look at Rational Emotive Therapy

Hmm, I'm still pissed off, but we can reuse a lot of the work we put into that proposal. And, we met some good people at Concorde and created a good impression. Who knows when they might pop up in our life again? Right, back to work, let's get on with it.

Rationalising fundamentally alters your definition of failure. Failure is just another experience. It deserves no more credit than that. What is critical is *what you do after failing*. You have two choices: give up, or use the experience to help you shape the path ahead.

Giving up is always an option, but consider the ramifications. Your last act in business was to fail and surrender. And you accepted this. The word "loser" springs to mind.

Think about this if you are considering giving up. Is this the *last* setback you will be dealt in life?

No way. So when the next one happens, are you just going to give up again? If you do, there will soon be nothing left, no more fuel in the tank. Dead. A miserable future beckons. You die before you die.

So really, there is no choice but to move on. And why not do it with a wry smile on your face, instead of an agonised grimace? The world looks infinitely more promising.

The past is gone, the future is the only thing. Get up and keep going, even when it looks impossible.

> **"It always seems impossible until it's done." (Nelson Mandela)**

Key points

- Trying new things builds self-esteem—the lifeblood of self-belief. You can do anything you want, if you believe in yourself.
- Not everything goes the way you want it to. It is the nature of life. Get over it and get on with it.
- Failure is just another experience, not the end of the world. It all depends on what you tell yourself about the experience.
- Refuse to let your defeats discourage you. Laugh about it, use what you can from it and move on.
- You're dead for a long time. You might as well be positive while you're alive. The alternative is pretty depressing.

The Snake Oil Salesman's view "Oh yeah, right! All this warm and fuzzy 'let's learn from the experience' drivel. There's no room for failure in my business, I just scare and confuse my customers so much they have to buy. Life is crap, and then you die."

CHAPTER 3

Starting out in selling— the wonder years

"It's not for us to wonder why, it's but for us to flog and fly."
(Delboy's philosophy towards selling and customer service,
from the British comedy series, Only Fools and Horses)

The following case study is my own story and how I fell into making a classic mistake when starting out in sales. Learn from my mistake and avoid looking like a fool.

Case Study 2: Self-destruction in 9 Words

I started my sales career in a US bank in Sydney, Australia. I knew nothing about banking, having spent the first five years of my career in the Australian Public Service. I was running training courses such as customer service and orientation for new starters in the Tax Office.

After scores of interviews with the private sector I finally landed a new job, head of Consumer Bank training. Two years later the national sales manager offered me a job. He said that I had the right personality for sales. We were a new bank in Australia with no market share and we needed someone to "get our foot in the door".

They were exciting times. This was the first time foreign banks were allowed to operate in Australia and compete in the domestic market. Customers were interested to learn about what the foreign banks could offer.

So it was a lot of cold-calling to start with. My job was to call organisations that collected lots of cheques. Public utilities, insurance companies, credit card businesses and government agencies were all on our hit list. We had a great product for processing these cheques. It helped the customers cut costs and increase revenue.

It was a no-brainer. My job was to ring up these organisations and make appointments. We only had one competitor and they were behind the eight-ball compared to us technology-wise.

As my boss said: "You don't need to know any details, there's plenty of guys here who know how the system works. Your job is to get us in the door."

I made the appointment, went along to the meeting, was friendly and said nothing. After the meeting I would ask our secretary to retrieve the last proposal, change the customer name and address and send it. Because we had decided to go in hard and offer the cheapest prices, we won most of the business.

It was a great first year and I was on my way.

Into the second year my boss, Rick, decided it was time to broaden my horizons. The bank was starting to do some solid business with the multinational corporate (MNC) sector. We needed to *leverage* these relationships, because there were "multi-product opportunities".

I didn't really know what this meant, being a "single-product guy". But Rick's plan was to arrange joint client meetings with the Relationship Managers in charge of the MNCs and I would go along to "learn the ropes".

I was quite intimidated to begin with. I had no idea how companies worked. I lived in fear of being asked any questions by the customer. After a while I learned enough to give a high-level overview of our part of the bank but I had no real substance or relevant experience to draw upon.

Rick showed a lot of faith in me and was very encouraging. After all, my sales revenue for Year One was pretty impressive.

So we were meeting this high-profile client with one of the Relationship Managers. Rick agreed with Steve, the Relationship Manager, that it would be good practice for me to open the meeting. It was with one of the world's biggest computer companies, a household name then, as it is now.

I was petrified at this initiation into the corporate world. The boardroom, the dark suits, power ties, expensive shirts and cufflinks, the astonishing view of Sydney Harbour. The rugby, horseracing and sailing banter. For the past 12 months I'd spent most of my time discussing cheque volumes with cardigan-clad mailroom clerks in the basement of run-down government offices.

Highly intimidating. The old-boys club. Private schools and university degrees. All smiles and handshakes. I was as out of place as a New Guinea highlander at the controls of the space shuttle.

After the small talk, it was clearly time to get to the business. Rick looked at me expectantly and nodded. Clearing my throat, I tried to look confident and introduced our team, thanking the client for their time. Good start.

"So gentlemen", I said, leaning forward and trying to look serious, assertive and business-like, "what kind of business are you in?" (Self-destruction in 9 words)

The clients didn't know if I was joking or not. The three of them looked bemused, shocked or contemptuous. My colleagues were equally stunned. You could have heard a cockroach fart. Thankfully, my boss was a quick thinker and came to the rescue.

"Ahem, Bernie's quite new to this industry. He has a great track record selling to government." Rick made a bit of a joke about my huge faux pas, rolling his eyes theatrically.

Looking at me with feigned annoyance, he said: "What you were supposed to ask is—what is the main business priority for the Printer Division this year?"

We all had a bit of a nervous, dubious laugh at this lame cover-up. I accepted the lifeline gratefully and nodded as if that was indeed what I meant to say.

"Yes, yes, sorry, ahh . . . the Printing Division." I somehow managed to raise my eyebrows inquiringly, almost choking with fear as I looked directly at the corporate treasurer. "Yes Jeff, ah, the targets this year . . . ?"

My pen was poised as I looked earnestly at Jeff, praying for a positive response. I tried to imagine myself as a financial consultant taking confidential notes, sitting with industry leaders over cocktails and cigars at the Sydney Club. Thankfully, Jeff took pity on me and gave me a few comments. I feverishly scribbled them into my book.

"Thanks very much Jeff, that's very helpful," I said pitifully, putting my pen down and effectively ending my involvement in the meeting.

There was no hole big enough for me to hide in—it was humiliating. The clients ignored me and got on with things, and a good discussion ensued.

Naturally I played no part in that. I just sat there nodding and trying to look intelligent. I kept my trap shut, remembering the saying "it's better to keep your mouth shut and look a fool, than open your mouth and remove all doubt". It's just a pity I didn't think of that before I started the meeting.

I could not wait for the embarrassing charade to be over. Once we got out of the lift the Relationship Manager glared at me disdainfully and said: "You can forget coming on another call with me—that was disgraceful! I would be amazed if they ever wanted to see you again!"

Harsh words, but true. It was humiliating. But Rick was great. He took full responsibility. He said to the Relationship Manager: "I know it was a very poor start Steve and I apologise for that. But it's not Bernie's fault, it's mine. I should have spent more time briefing him before we left the office. It won't happen again."

Steve was still fuming. "Well if you want us to work together, sort your act out. I will have to call the client now and apologise for our complete lack of professionalism. They weren't impressed, I can tell you."

Rick took me to a pub, his favorite environment for coaching and team-building.

We sat there and mapped out a plan. For the next eight weeks I was to spend three hours in the morning researching the clients we were visiting that afternoon. Their business structure, their presence in Australia, their international profile, the products, the competition, who their bankers were and any relevant newspaper articles. I was to prepare a 10-minute presentation on each one before lunch and then we would plan the meeting flow.

I improved steadily as my confidence grew. Before long I was participating actively in the meetings as if I knew what we were all talking about. It was a bit of a smokescreen but half the battle is looking confident.

So that was my first lesson in selling. Be prepared. Investigate. Find out as much as you can before the meeting. Don't waste everyone's time asking about things you should know. With the internet, there is no excuse!

And by the way, the Relationship Manager, Steve, and I crossed paths some six months after our ill-fated first encounter. He called me and said: "Rick has asked me to take you to the IBM meeting. Let me ask you something before I agree. Tell me what you know about IBM. You can start with what the letters IBM stand for." The sarcasm was palpable.

Luckily I had all my notes right in front of me, fresh from the morning's study session. "How much time have you got?" I asked him. I gave him a five-minute description of IBM's business in Australia, the extent of our bank's relationship and where I thought the treasury management opportunities could be.

He was impressed and even asked me to speak at the meeting. Amazing! We practised it in the taxi on the way there. He was a hard coach but he knew his customer well. He did not want a repeat performance of the first debacle.

He said: "I have been working with this client for 10 years. I know the guys and the company inside-out. I get invited to the CEO's kids' birthdays. He and I play golf every Sunday at Royal Sydney. He gives me first crack at every bit of business they have on offer. I don't need some lazy ex-public servant screwing up this relationship because you couldn't be bothered preparing. Got it?"

I got it. I could see it. I could feel it. I have never felt so much pressure as I did in that taxi. I really wished I was back in Canberra running the orientation course and having a laugh with all the freshly recruited public servants. But there was no turning back now. I was on the hook to perform.

"You have 10 minutes", Steve instructed me. "Explain the broad opportunity you foresee, based on your research of the company. I tend to agree it's a good one. Then give your example of how 'a competitor' of theirs is using the system and the benefits they are reaping. That will get them interested—they hate competitors. Then ask for permission to work with someone to analyse some numbers to prepare a cost-benefit analysis. They love numbers—they're accountants and engineers. And don't worry, I'll be able to back you up if they ask any tricky questions. Go for it!"

The meeting was positive and I survived. We got approval to go ahead and crunch some numbers. He punched me encouragingly in the arm as we left the meeting. We called in to a local pub for a beer to debrief.

He said: "I know I gave you a really hard time after that first meeting but, boy, did you deserve it. You remember John, the Treasurer? Well, when I rang him afterwards to apologise he just laughed at me. Every time I have called him for a meeting since, he's asked if you can come too, for entertainment value.

"And whenever I have seen those other guys out socially, they would ask, 'Where's Bernie?' Someone else would ask, 'Who's Bernie?' and the story would get told again, to everyone's disbelief and amusement. You were famous mate, for all the wrong reasons."

Still embarrassing now as I write these words, decades later.

Steve slapped me on the back and told me not to worry about it, it was a good lesson. He even paid for the beer in respect to the homework I had done on IBM.

"That was a great effort today", he said, "far better than I expected. By the way Jeff was talking, we may well have an opportunity in your area. You never know, we might even make a proper salesman out of you yet."

It was a great feeling. I knew then I was in the right game—the same one I am in today.

Death of the Snake Oil Salesman

And that is why this book is called *Death of the Snake Oil Salesman*. Because when you work as a partner, trying to ensure both sets of interests are met, you tend to win the business most of the time. Selling is fun, challenging and eminently rewarding if you see it as a two-way street.

You won't win every deal you work on. If it were that easy, everyone would be in sales. But by using the approach outlined in *Death of the Snake Oil Salesman* you give yourself the best fighting chance.

In each chapter you can steadily learn how to create value for the customer. There is a rationale for each step and lots of snippets—appalling and good—from my own and others' careers to illustrate the steps and the skills.

Death of the Snake Oil Salesman—people respond positively when they feel you have their interests at heart.

Key points

- Allocate one hour a day to looking at your prospects, otherwise your business will struggle. Plan an individual approach by researching them. Your business grows. It's as simple as that.
- Do your homework—know about your clients' business. There are many sources of information: websites, online news, newspapers and business magazines. Browse these every day.
- Look at the existing relationship between your business and the clients. Dig into the Client Relationship Management system. What is the history? What is the relationship like? Past deals and achievements? Talk to your colleagues who have ongoing dealings with the client in other countries and locations. Ask people you know who work with the company about the current business environment.

- Look at the industry in which your client operates. What's happening in the political, economic and social environments, for example currency volatility, change of government, social unrest? Think about how these factors may impact your client. Ask your colleagues their opinions. Be prepared to discuss these with your client.

- With all this preparation, develop some intelligent questions to ask your client. For example, how does the depreciation of the yen impact your customers. In other countries we have seen depreciation severely impact individual's buying power. Are you seeing this trend as well? What measures is your company taking to mitigate the business impact?

- Phrase your questions in fewer than 15 words. Practise asking them with your colleagues. Clients have more access to information today and lower attention spans. Don't make it sound like an interrogation.

- Plan the meeting. Send an agenda in advance. Be clear what you want to get out of it. Be clear on what the customer should get out of it.

- As my great friend Jason Wagner says—ya gotta consider the five P's—Prior Planning Prevents Poor Performance

Sample meeting preparation form:

Client.....................

Business....................

Turnover (global) .... (regional) .... (country by country)

Countries of Operation

Head Office

Organisation structure—main business lines

Their competitors

Existing client relationship with our firm

Recent deals / mandates / engagements

Key relationships: Roberto Mancini: Global Head of Procurement

Key Supporters

Recent news impacting the client—Political, Social, Economic

Possible challenges faced

Key questions to ask

Our competitors

Best possible meeting outcome: for the client / for us

The Snake Oil Salesman's view of this chapter: "What a load of bollocks! Don't waste your time with all of this admin. You just wing it on the day. When you've been around as long as I have, there's nothing new! You could write my meeting plan on the back of a cigarette packet."

CHAPTER 4

Developing a client relationship

The expert

It's always great to meet an expert, especially a self-proclaimed one who likes to talk about themselves. You get a free sales training lesson every time. Observe them carefully and write down everything they do. They will think you are carefully documenting their words of wisdom. When they have finished talking, thank them for their insights. Review your notes, and promise yourself you will do the complete opposite of what they did. You can't go wrong.

Selling isn't about you. It's about the person you are talking to.

Why do customers buy?

People become prospective customers because they have needs not being fulfilled by their current supply of goods and services. This could mean buying a new clock because the existing one is broken. The transaction is relatively low in value compared to buying a car, a house, or a unit trust investment. While some thought goes into buying the new clock, it is a short-lived experience. Therefore, the decision to buy is based mainly on product features and price.

The personality of the individual who sold it to you, or the degree to which they listen to your needs, is relatively unimportant. You buy the clock and move on. But as the value of the purchasing decision increases, so does the importance of the relationship skills of the seller.

Trust is increasingly important in the decision-making process as the buying risk grows. This is because the potential downside is greater. The more money we are spending, the more we take into account the credibility of the person we are dealing with.

Do we trust them sufficiently to handle the transaction and do everything that they say they will do?

In major transactions, any mistakes in the process can have financial implications. That is why customers take time before they buy. They make decisions when they trust the person they are dealing with—and when they understand the value of the deal. Sometimes they need the approval of other people before they can give you the business.

The client also needs to feel assured you will respond quickly when there are problems. In essence, they have to *believe* the person selling the service. Belief is fundamental to trust. It takes time to build up. The buyer begins to trust the seller who is trying to help them and whom they think has their interests at heart.

One of the reasons salespeople lose deals is they try to close too quickly. They offer products blindly instead of listening to problems and finding solutions. This approach implies to the client that the seller is only interested in themself and meeting their targets.

Case Study 3: Blowing the deal

I'm sitting in one of my favorite pubs in Singapore with my friend Sule, waiting for lunch. He's Jordanian, a funds manager. The restaurant manager walks over and introduces herself, Claudette. She is an Aussie, so we have some common ground. She asks me about the service in the pub.

I say, "It's usually OK, but not that great."

She says, "Right, what can we do?"

That moment our lunch arrives, interrupting our discussion. There was no greeting, no smile, just an unhappy person dishing up our lunch. She dumps the plates, grunts, snorts and leaves.

"Well I'd start with sacking that miserable cow, if I was you," I offer. "There are at least five pubs within one minute of here that sell fish and chips for lunch. It's not as though this is the best. I mean, it's nice but let's face it, it's fish and chips. And that person who just dumped the food on our table? Well, on what planet did you find her? It's like she hates us"

Claudette is rightfully horrified by the indifferent nature of her waitress. She apologises profusely and disappears. Within minutes she is back at our table with three bottles of Tiger.

"Gents, I'm really sorry about that. I will deal with it. I agree that was terrible. It's so difficult to get good customer service staff here.

"Look, it's no excuse—lunch is on the house. I'm so sorry, I can't believe she did that. Thanks for having lunch here today. It's my shout."

We are impressed by Claudette's service recovery—free beer is better than nothing, in any country. She sits down and we clink glasses.

"So what are you guys doing in Singapore?" Claudette asks the standard question.

"I'm a funds manager," Sule says.

I say: "I'm a training consultant, and I know we can help you in your business. The person who served our lunch was terrible. She had no interpersonal skills. She couldn't care less about us. We can make a big difference with your customer service. We run customer service training courses and we are recognised as the best in the business. We have global contracts with some of the world's biggest companies. We have a customer with similar issues and we have made a huge difference . . . blah, blah, blah, blah, blah . . ."

Claudette didn't respond as I thought she would. I expected her to jump out of her seat and embrace me, as if was the very saviour she had been waiting for. It was obvious to me. The service was shit and we did great customer service training. And we were both Australians—we understood. We would get on like a house on fire. It was a done deal. When do we start?

Instead of expressing her undying gratitude, she acknowledged my comments, wiped her hands on her apron. "Well, that's really good to know Bernie, thank you. I'll let you know if we can do with your help."

It wasn't the response I expected. I immediately pulled my card out of my pocket. "Great Claudette, thanks very much for the beers. Um, why don't we meet and talk about this some more. We are great at customer service training. We've worked around the world, especially Asia."

She smiled at me and took my card. "Thanks Bernie." She dipped behind the bar for one of hers. "Sorry, I've run out. Look, I better go, I've got a big group coming in for lunch. Nice to meet you. Bye."

Uncovering customer needs

Did we get the deal? No way. I blew it, big time. These guys have 20 pubs in Singapore and I blew it.

Why?

I went in too hard, too early. I didn't take the time to understand how the business works, the job roles, the customer profile, the pressures, the timing, the responsibilities, nothing. I just jumped in without understanding anything, saying, "We can fix it". I had established no credibility, nothing—just some Product-Pushing Snake Oil Salesman with a hammer who thinks everything looks like a nail.

> *"There is nothing more dangerous than a great idea, if it's your only one" (Anonymous)*

I blew the restaurant training deal because I was excited. Would we have made the difference if we had have trained the team? Absolutely, I have no doubt. But we weren't even in with a chance because I made the customer feel like she was the same as everyone else. She wasn't special. We deal with this stuff all the time. We'll just apply the same *solution* we applied to the customer service team at the dental clinic we trained last week. You're all the same.

In making a decision that will impact her business, Claudette wanted someone to understand her specific needs and who was focused on helping her achieve her objectives. I failed that test immediately—and miserably.

The seller must uncover the customer's true needs. This is achieved through a structured consultative process.

Key points

- The key to selling is showing interest in your client. When you are talking about your product, ask yourself "why am I talking?". Is it to help the client, or is to help yourself? If it's the latter, stop talking and ask another question. Then clarify what you understand.
- Many products are "commodities", pretty much the same from one vendor to another. Some examples are building, insurance, chemicals, personal investment and pharmaceutical products. Hotels, restaurants and conference centres often sit in the same field. In these cases, if you are Product-Pushing, there is Big Squeeze on price for you to get the deal, because they can't see the *value*. You differentiate yourself from the Snake Oil Salesman by learning about client's needs and matching your product features and benefits accordingly.

- Asking questions before giving solutions is the *number one skill* in selling. It requires a conscious thought process to *shut up and listen.* As you find out more information, think to yourself: "What did I just learn? What do I not understand about what I just learnt?" Then find out more.

- Wait for the client to ask you what you can do. This is a clear sign they are interested in your capabilities. Avoid firing off solutions too early (Product-Pushing). It shows desperation and looks like you aren't really interested in that clients' challenges. It sounds like you are already calculating the revenue from the deal. Not good.

- All customers want to feel special, that they are different. And why not? They are.

**The Snake Oil Salesman's view:
"I'm a Mover & Shaker. I
haven't got time to dilly-dally.
Sure, ask a couple of questions
to pretend you're interested.
Nod in agreement. Look
concerned. Prove you're an
expert by telling them what
they're doing wrong. Give
them the solution—they
expect that. Then change the
name on the last proposal and
send it out to them. They'll
never know."**

CHAPTER 5

Death of the Snake Oil Salesman

The Sales Partner demonstrates they are interested in a mutually beneficial relationship with the client. They do this by learning about the client's objectives and then helping to meet those objectives.

They ask thoughtful questions and listen attentively. The client wants ideas that help them meet their needs—both short-term (current needs) and in the future (anticipated needs). The Sales Partner only starts thinking about appropriate solutions if they understand these needs.

By asking questions—and listening—the Sales Partner demonstrates a desire to understand the client and their position. They try to understand the problems that are impacting on the client achieving their objectives. A salesperson who tries to sell products without relating the benefits to the client's objectives is not helping them.

Clients are interested in solutions that address *their* problems. The Sales Partner's job is to uncover these issues. Sometimes there are needs of which the client may not be aware. She is able to help the client become aware of these by sharing product knowledge and industry experience.

The value of the IMPACT model

Customers have vastly differing experiences, situations and goals. To start offering products without knowing anything about the client's personal situation is spraying and praying. That should be a clear warning sign they are locked in the sights of the Snake Oil Salesman's shotgun.

So how do you change that? Use the IMPACT model.

INVESTIGATE their interests

MAP out their processes and obstacles

PRIORITISE their needs

ASK what they want to change

CONFIRM you listened

TAILOR the solution.

It's about creating value.
Are you improving your customer's life?

Key points

- Concentrate on what's important to the client, not you.
- Research in advance of meetings—information is the currency of negotiation.
- Avoid going in with the solution in mind. It will definitely affect your objectivity. Position yourself as a problem-solver, genuinely interested in helping your client.
- Maintain objectivity during the meeting, especially when you can see the deal you had in mind is of no interest to the client.
- Don't try to bring the meeting discussion back to your needs (to close the deal). Force yourself to focus on their needs.
- Use the IMPACT model to prepare the meeting flow. It makes sense and gives you a framework to manage the conversation. The next chapters cover each step in detail, with some classic examples and some reliable questions to ask.

The client-focused "Trusted Financial Adviser"

The Snake Oil Salesman's view on this chapter.

"You've got to be kidding! Asking the clients questions?! Waste of time! That's what <u>they</u> pay <u>me</u> for! Clients love me because I know what's going on in the market. They want me to tell them about our great products, and do a 'special deal' for them". That's how you make people feel special. We are operating in the real world—close the deal! Always be closing! Theoretical models belong in some classroom. You won't see me in some wanky sales training course—haven't got time—I'm out there, on the road, doing deals."

CHAPTER 6

Investigate client interests

Find out as much as you can before the meeting. Solid preparation saves a lot of time in the initial meeting with the client. As well as being impressed with your preparation, the client will be able to validate information you have rather than finding it and getting back to you. This also creates a favourable first impression. Don't ask the same questions that have been asked a hundred times before. That's poor form, it's unprofessional and it makes you look like "just another Snake Oil Salesman".

I once asked the CFO of a petroleum company in Jakarta, "Would you mind telling me how many petrol stations you have across the country?" He said: "Why don't you look in the Call Report your colleague should have written six months ago when he asked the same question? Nothing's changed. In fact, I am quite busy. Come back and see me in a few months when you have done some research."

Case study 4: The expert

Before I became a Snake Oil Salesman, I headed the training department for Consumer Banking. We were setting the training agenda for the year ahead. My colleague Choon, and I had met a lot of people in the bank, who all had their views on what was needed. We had much of the content covered—teamwork, customer service, orientation, frontline supervision—the basics. But our big need was senior executive training. I knew nothing about this and nor did Choon.

After all, we were ex-public servants up against some heavyweights in the finance industry. Talk about being out of your depth. I couldn't even work out how to balance my chequebook, let alone train senior bankers in leadership skills. So, we called for help. We put the feelers out. Next thing, we have a meeting with some guy from a prominent Australian business school.

I am yet to meet a more arrogant bastard than this guy.

Some background:

- We had a budget of AUD100,000 to spend on leadership development training, in the first year. This is 1988. That money is now worth around AUD250,000.
- There were four prospective suppliers, and we had to get the best.
- We didn't really know what we were talking about.

I go to the meeting in our head office. We sit in Choon's office, waiting for the salesman to turn up. He was late and gave some excuse about buses running behind schedule. Even I, the ex-public servant, thought that this was a little ordinary. After all, I had spent my previous five years feeding that bullshit to my boss in the public service.

The expert, Shane, arrived. He apologised, to his credit. He gave his presentation. It was self-centred, boring and long-winded.

Shane, the Snake Oil Salesman, said: "Our research shows that senior managers need to be selling more. They need selling skills, they need to be more in touch with their customers. They need to listen more. They need to understand that the world is changing, that customers expect a more ubiquitous value proposition where traditional borders of commerce and politics are challenged, and their subordinates are driven by the same value chain."

I had no idea what he was talking about. I felt like an idiot. This new world that I was operating in was very difficult to understand. What did it mean? Why is the business world so hard to understand?

Choon asked him a question. "Excuse me Shane, but how does this fit in to our senior executive training program?" I wanted to ask the same question, but was too scared. I eagerly anticipated Shane's response. Which was: "You guys have no idea of what lies ahead of you. You are seriously out of your depth. We are the experts in this field and you best leave it to us."

I didn't know what to say then, either, and thankfully Choon again came to the rescue.

"But what exactly are you proposing Shane? We need to deliver a proposal to the Executive Committee to show them how we will train the top guys in leadership skills. So far, we haven't seen anything we can use."

Shane huffed and checked his watch, clearly running out of patience with the imbeciles he was dealing with. It seemed that we were a complete waste of his time and he had bigger fish to fry elsewhere.

"Look you guys, I have been in this industry for a lot longer than you, don't forget that. We are experts in this field of executive training. I am studying for my PhD, so I think I know what I'm talking about. Put the money on the table and then we can talk. Look, I've got to go. Here's my card. Call me when you know what you want to do and when you have the budget. Which way is the lift?"

So that was the end of the meeting. I was really glad when Choon got up out of his chair and said, "Well that's really helpful Shane, thank you . . . let me show you the way out".

Enormously relieved, I got up too and walked out to the lift lobby with Choon and Shane. Someone pressed the button and after what seemed an eternity, the lift arrived. Shane stepped in, looking at his Rolodex, annoyed that he was running late for his next client. Just as the lift doors were closing, he turned and looked at us, pointing his finger.

"I make heroes out of guys like you."

The doors closed and he was gone. Thank Christ. Choon and I looked at each other, stunned by this encounter. Then we laughed our heads off. What a dickhead! That idiot Shane had just left the premises of a company that had one hundred grand to spend, and we never wanted to see him again. He blew it. He didn't ask us one single question. He had no idea who we were or what we were doing. He couldn't have cared less. But, he was The Expert—he didn't need to know.

People buy from people

All Shane needed to do was his homework. If he bothered, he would have a lot of information at his disposal that he could have used to impress us, such as:

- The fact that we were representing the biggest US bank, which spends a fortune on training.
- What the other banks were doing and how we could benefit from this information.
- Where the banking market was going and how important executive leadership training was to success.
- What would happen if we didn't provide excellent training to these senior guys.
- Examples of his other work, how it had helped other companies with the same issues and how that might fit into our plans.
- Then, if he had earned the right to ask us questions by demonstrating his homework, he would have found out:
  - ❖ We had a budget of 100 grand to spend on his company, in the first year.
  - ❖ Our three-year budget was AUD3 million.
  - ❖ If successful, we could replicate the business deal in to a multi-million deal within five years around the region. And who knows? After that, the sky is the limit, as they say.

Shane's problem was he did no *Investigation*. He assumed his product would suit us. Just like everyone else. And if it didn't, well, we were idiots. He was the original Spray & Pray man. I thank him for the magnificent insight he gave me into the game of selling.

The reason Shane screwed it up? He walked into the game thinking he'd already won it. He probably had us down on his prospect list as a "done deal". But he failed to realise something important: *people buy from people*. It doesn't matter how great your product is. If you think 'I am the same as everyone else', you can walk out that door now. Show some respect. Do your homework.

Know something about me before you walk in the door. Investigate, and then ask me questions about what I'm interested in. Clarify the client's interests—it's not that hard to do. And I appreciate the effort. I want to talk with you. Then we are off and running.

By investigating before the meeting he would have impressed us with his preparation. All clients feel they are special and have individual needs. No one likes to feel they are the same as the rest of the pack. By asking us about what we have been doing, he learns about our interests and priorities. What is happening now? He would have discovered we indeed had a need for his services. Instead, we never wanted to see him again. Bye Shane, good luck in the next life!

Snake Oil Salesmen should be taken outside and shot with minimal fuss.

Key points

Here's what Shane could have done to create a great impression. He could have:

- Shown he had some knowledge about the bank. "The bank has been operating now for three years and has already made some significant impact in the market."
- Shown interest in Choon and I. "It would be good to learn more about your background—would you mind telling what you specialise in?" With sites like LinkedIn, you've got everything you need.
- Find some common ground. "I've been involved in a similar field. It will be good to share some stories and exercises."
- Asked about the work we have done since joining the bank.
- Asked what conclusions we had arrived at, and review our summary of findings.
- Asked about our objectives, what we are measured on.
- Asked what we felt we could cover through internal resources and where we were looking for assistance.

"I keep six honest serving-men, they taught me all I knew; Their names are What and Why and When And How and Where and Who." (Rudyard Kipling)

The Snake Oil Salesman's view: "Like, who's got time for all of this? I've said it before and I'll say it again—selling is a numbers game. I'd be lucky to have two appointments a day with this 'model bullshit' approach. Right now I average eight. In and out mate, that's what its all about. Making money. Move on to the next sucker—err, sorry, client"

CHAPTER 7

Map the processes and obstacles

"The most important skill in selling is taking notes," the Sales Director told me when I started. I found that difficult to understand. I thought selling was all about talking, convincing people. I didn't realise that you are more likely to earn trust by listening. Even now, 25 years later, it's still hard to stop talking and just shut up. Imagine *you* are the only person who finds your opinion interesting. That's a bit of a shock.

Stop talking, ask questions, listen and take notes.

Is selling about convincing people to buy something, or helping improve their business and their life? Your answer to this question determines your approach. If you know your products will improve your customers' business, you need to know where they fit in, what challenges they address and how they change things for the better.

For you to know how you fit in, you must know what happens now and how it happens. This is called Mapping.

Case study 4: The Mapping Master

My colleague Warren and I visited the Singapore HQ of a global petroleum company. I met two women there—the Regional Treasurer and the Cash Manager They told me quite contentedly their Asia cash management was in safe hands with their banker. They used this bank everywhere in the world. I asked them what they meant by safe hands. They told me that this bank was saving them money, it was a great deal.

I said: "I don't want to waste your time, or mine. In this region there are many problems with collecting and reconciling money, particularly in a business that has thousands of distributors and petrol stations in remote places. The most difficult countries are Indonesia, India, Thailand, China and the Philippines."

I produced a chart showing all their petrol stations and distributors throughout Asia, highlighting the difficult countries.

"Where did you get this from?" asked the Treasurer, intrigued by the chart I taped on to the whiteboard.

"Warren is responsible for this. He is the Master Mapper of business processes. He's over here from the US helping us, and he pulled this together."

"Thanks Bern," Warren chimed in with the baritone voice.

"Most of it I got from internal bank files, the internet and your annual report. I'm not sure if it's accurate and I want to check that with you. But if you give me a minute I'd just like to open some discussion about how things work right now. Is that OK?"

"Sure" they both said, glued to the map, after fleetingly exchanging surprised, impressed, raised eyebrows.

"Thank you. OK, what you can see is you have 7300 petrol stations in Indonesia, spread across the islands. Some of these are owned by the company and others are franchised. You have four depots. You have at least 500 petrol tankers driving around Indonesia at any time. They deliver the petrol and drop off the invoice and pick up the cheques for the last delivery.

"From our knowledge of other petrol companies, it usually takes about four weeks for those cheques to be banked. So they lose all of that interest. And when the credit hits their account, Accounts Receivable can't work out who paid, how much they paid, and what they paid for. It's all reported manually on paper about one to two weeks later. And because there are many disputed invoices, it's impossible to reconcile money coming in.

"This means the accounting department doesn't know how much money has come in, when it's coming in and, when it does come in, who it belongs to. What this implies is the petrol stations that have paid are not recognised, so we hold up supplying them again. They complain but the petrol company can't do anything about it because they don't know for certain if the customer *has* paid.

"Reminder notices are sent out to customers who have already paid, which is bad for the company image. There are multiple flow-on effects creating inefficiency and escalating costs in working capital. In our experience, almost 50% of working capital is locked up in these historical collection practices. Is this happening in your company?"

Warren paused while Celia and Ting Gue stared at the map.

Ting Gue was the first to break. She gave a giggle, quite common in Asia when people are nervous.

"It sounds like us," she said candidly, "What do you propose?"

There is no greater breakthrough than having a clinical, analytical client ask your opinion.

We had a strategy.

"We'd like to go to there and map out the process," I said. "We'll map out the steps and quantify the cost to Energy Inc. Then we will know what the current costs and risks are and whether it's worthwhile changing anything. It may be acceptable risk and it may not. But we don't know yet."

"How much will that cost us?" asked Celia, who was clearly warming up to the opportunity. We gave our fee, time and expenses and Celia duly accepted it. She gave us their India operations as our test case.

So there we were. Sitting on the plane together, en route to India. Me, the Master Mapper Warren, and Celia, the Regional Treasurer. A trip through India, to unravel the intricacies of the cash management practices of Energy Inc with thousands of petrol stations, awaited. Our first stop was the main depot in Chennai, a sprawling city teeming with life, noise, bustling traffic, colour and pungent smells.

Celia accompanied us at the meeting, where we met the depot manager, a portly, important looking chap named Pradeep. He sat back in his large executive chair, looking quizzically at the ensemble before him. A nervous young fellow knocked and entered, skilfully balancing a tray of tea, coffee, biscuits, cups, milk and sugar.

"Well Pradeep," Celia said, "Bern and Warren are helping us review our treasury management practices. I'd like to understand how things work here in India, from the ordering process through to the banking. We'll appreciate your co-operation. Bern will outline the proposal."

I stood up and thanked Pradeep for his time. "Pradeep, the first thing I want to say is we are here to understand the business. We have done our homework but need to validate what we know. Would it be OK if we spend some time with your accounting team?"

Pradeep made a phone call and a tall man with a magnificent moustache materialised. Ranjeev, head of depot operations. He warmly welcomed us and took us to another part of the office. We spent the next five hours in a cavernous, warm, whitewashed office with desks and chairs carefully arranged for the group of 20 or so accounting clerks, all smiling nervously.

A large, noisy overhead fan was groaning tiredly at half-tilt. There were five or six large boxes overflowing with paper on a long sorting table. Documents were carefully arranged in neat stacks along the breadth and width of the bench top.

Warren stood up and took over. "Here's what we do team," he announced, in his gravelly voice. "We start from the beginning. And we ain't leavin' here until we get to the end."

Then he started—every single step of the process from ordering to reconciliation of payment was mapped out over a tortuous seven-hour period, breaking only for a 30-minute lunch. Warren flowcharted every step of the process on the whiteboard, asking questions and quantifying steps and actions. It was like a murder investigation. But it turned up nothing. We couldn't find any glaring cracks in the process. Disappointed, we thanked the guys for their efforts, and headed to a nearby bar to buy Ranjeev a beer. Then, the breakthrough.

"I didn't want to say this publicly," Ranjeev said cautiously, "but it occurred to me today where the problem is. Going through that process had me wondering and now I realise it. Our bank has ripping us off for years. We are paying . . ." and then went into intricate detail about some receivables financing deal, which the previous Treasurer (some dodgy expat) had struck some years ago with his friend at the bank.

Ranjeev produced some old and new banking statements and contracts. Warren studied the first page like a forensic expert. He flicked through a few more, nodding his head with a spreading, wicked grin on his face. It turned out their bank was charging for a service that cost more than it earned. By about USD 1 million per annum, for doing nothing.

The next morning over breakfast we discussed the findings with Celia. She called Pradeep to tell him to be available at nine o'clock for a meeting. Pradeep looked mighty sheepish and a bit nervous. He pointed out quickly that this arrangement had been in place well before his appointment. It had "slipped through the cracks". Celia was not impressed. "So Pradeep, can you please check that— we are paying 1 million a year for something we don't use? Is that right? I'd like an answer in an hour."

Celia then asked us to study the payments process as well.

Warren sat all the Accounts Payable staff in a room and hosted a competition. "What would be the easiest way to defraud this company?" was his opening question. We flip-charted all of the responses and put them on a map. Within one hour we found it—a big security breach. The "fully automated" payment pipeline had a manual step in it, allowing changes to be made in payment details. This meant anyone who had access to the system could make a payment to themselves and approve it. Celia was horrified.

The cosy relationship between Pradeep and Celia was suddenly quite frosty. The smiles and banter disappeared, and Celia called an emergency meeting with the senior management committee.

Warren and I had done our job and it was time to leave. We said our goodbyes and received a filthy look from Pradeep. I think Ranjeev was probably the only one who was sorry we were leaving. We went back to the hotel and wrote the report with accompanying process maps. Our finding was they could save more than USD2 million in collection costs by changing their bank and that they had potential for up to USD10 million in fraudulent payments unless they fixed the system.

Yet, despite all of this work we were never awarded the business. Energy Inc. could not appoint a new bank in India—but they put their existing banker to the torch. Three months later Celia moved to a new company. She contacted me and asked to repeat the process with Warren in the new firm. She gave us her commitment to award us the business wherever we found problems. Twelve months later we had become that company's regional bank, earning more than USD1 million a year in fees.

Key points

- Get close to the customer's business by doing your research. Work with your colleagues to understand how the business flows. If you don't have this resource in-house, find people in your network to help you.
- Develop the ability to write clearly on a whiteboard or flipcharts. It demonstrates confidence and puts you into problem-solving mode. There is no discussion of solutions.
- Quantify every step of the process, where you can. Check each statement made to you.
- Summarise the process to your client's satisfaction. Document thoroughly. Create a flowchart and send it to your client for their validation.
- Write a report clearly quantifying the current practices and cost / revenue opportunities. Be conservative with your numbers. Share the report with your colleagues and ask them to poke holes in it.
- Send the DRAFT Findings to your client for review. Ask her about the next steps. Be guided by your customer. Don't push for something that may not be there.
- Keep in mind, you may not win this deal. There are many factors at work and people within the client organisation who will not want to see any changes made, for their own reasons.

The offer closes at 5 o'clock - let's shake on it now, you don't want to miss out

"So now you're telling me I've gotta be the psychiatrist as well as the surgeon! Get serious. All this warm fluffy soft skills rubbish is a waste of time. Whiteboards and Flipcharts? Seriously, what have you guys been smoking? I'm not a primary school teacher—I'm a Trusted Financial Advisor. How do I know? Coz I've been there and done it! Got the business and holiday home to prove it."

CHAPTER 8

Prioritise client needs

Steven Levitt talks about incentives in the excellent *Freakonomics*—social, moral and financial incentives. These are the drivers of our behaviour. I have come to the conclusion that selling is about helping other people achieve their financial incentives. These are normally articulated in the form of a Scorecard, or KPIs, or Performance Objectives. It sounds mercenary but it makes sense. Will implementing your product help me get a better rating or not?

My friend James, who was head of procurement at a large company, said to me: "I get measured on cost savings. My scorecard allocates 80% of my performance to reducing costs associated with telecoms, banking, insurance, travel and accommodation, IT hardware and software, and consulting fees. I tell every salesperson who comes to see me, 'Help me cut my costs and I will find a way to award you business. Don't come in and present products that are going to increase my costs. They might be interesting in their features, but those features don't benefit me. Help me achieve my scorecard and I will help you'."

I was stunned by the simplicity of this thinking.

James continued: "I have people asking me out for golf, dinner, meetings, wanting to bring this important guy to see me, all the time. I go to some of these, just to keep the relationship. But these activities are not valuable to me in any other way. They don't contribute positively to my scorecard. Hardly any of these people get the business, and I tell them why. 'You have to add value'."

Adding value

Adding value is one of these phrases that came out about 30 years ago and was jumped on by the consulting bandwagon. Most of the time it is thrown into the conversation or proposal along with vague terms like robust, scalable, sustainable, holistic, seamless and agile. There are hundreds of these words that don't mean anything on their own but they are used repeatedly in business by people who don't realise how unconvincing they sound when they use them.

Adding value, in my view, means helping someone achieve their incentives, their scorecard. If what I have helps you achieve your scorecard and I can prove it, why wouldn't you buy from me? It's logical. I add value to you by helping you cut your costs, or improve your quality, or increase your market share, or reduce your customer complaints, or whatever it is you get measured on.

If I am offering a service such as market entry strategies for Russia, or Portuguese translation consulting and you run a local supermarket in Ghana, you will most likely be uninterested as there's nothing in it for you. You may feel some moral or social incentive in helping me but unless these products contribute to your scorecard I won't get too far with you in the sales process.

Uncovering interests and priorities are fundamental to selling. Investigating and Mapping are the first two steps, Prioritising is next. And *my* priority is my scorecard.

Asking the questions is pretty easy. Once you've mapped out the process and quantified the obstacles and potholes, you can ask the question, "Which one is the priority?" The answer to that question will be directly linked to the person's scorecard.

"Hmm, let me see, if we tackle Issue A I am going to cut costs by 10%. If we tackle issue B I am going to double my revenue in 12 months. Cutting costs is a 5% item on my scorecard. Doubling revenue is number one, contributing 80% to my overall performance. No-brainer."

So while the proposal to cut costs may be a wonderful idea, it's not my priority. However, if the weighting for cutting costs was 80%, I would be much more interested.

Another way of looking at Priorities is the analogy of a time-bomb, sitting there ready to explode. The IMPACT process gives the client some time to think through the issues in their business and the challenges they are facing. If they don't do something about the identified problem it may possibly get worse. The client decides whether they can afford to let things continue to fester. If the *potential* outcome is unacceptable because of the negative impact on the scorecard it becomes a Priority.

The eternal struggle of the salesman is aligning his customers' priorities with his own. The salesman's priorities remain constant— win new business, grow the business. Customers are wired differently—they are measured on different things. And these incentives can change quickly.

Case study 6: The great chili crab cook-off

We'd come in late on a big deal. A large bank had shortlisted two vendors to design and deliver their Service Quality program. We weren't even part of the initial evaluation process—they didn't know about us and we didn't know about them. So it was a small miracle when, three months later, we were awarded the business. Our objective was clearly spelt out by our new client, who was certainly the most discerning we had encountered. The program had to be unique, memorable and change the service mindset of every one of the 2500 staff in the company.

"This has visibility, this project, and the CEO is sponsoring it— it's got to be effective," she told us, in a thinly veiled warning "I'm putting a lot of faith into you, don't screw it up!" was what she may as well have said.

We brainstormed how we would do this project—2500 people to be trained in customer service and apply the training afterwards in their jobs. We needed something memorable to kick it off with and we came up with the Great Chili Crab Cook-off. The idea was to invite several charity groups from Singapore to a big beach resort and have all of the staff cook chili crab, a local favourite, for them. It would be pitched as a Guinness Book of Records attempt, thereby guaranteeing a huge amount of interest from within the company and, of course, in the press. It would be fantastic publicity for all of the right reasons, as the banks weren't exactly the flavour of the month in the press, being the middle of the Global Financial Crisis.

We discussed this idea and got the green light to develop it into a proposal. I was travelling in Europe at the time for about three weeks on end so everything was pulled together remotely. There were a host of things to consider, the weather being the obvious vulnerability. We scheduled a presentation to the project team for a Wednesday evening. I spent the weekend in Holland preparing the presentation and emailing back and forth to the team. By Sunday afternoon it was finally ready and looked great—unique idea, corporate responsibility angle, maximum involvement, great publicity, the works.

We met the client and I started to present the Great Chili Crab Cook-off, confident this outrageous proposal would blow them away. But after about two or three minutes, our client, Maria, said: "Look we've been thinking about this idea. It sounds exciting and its got some great angles to it, but it's got risk written all over it. Let's face it, it could rain and then what? The CEO doesn't want to do it—it has way too much downside. And it's not really sustainable. Our priorities have changed. We have to think of something else."

I don't know what prepares you to just be able to adapt to this kind of news but I suspect years of running training courses enabled me to "seamlessly" change tack. Despite my disappointment I facilitated a brainstorming session with the people in the room.

Who were they, what were they interested in, what was their priority now and what would be a great solution? My colleagues madly filled flipcharts with comments until we had drained the room of ideas. The whole priority had changed. It was no longer the Big Bang extravaganza. It was to be a variety of sessions aimed at different levels, with variations in content for different parts of the business. It had to go beyond traditional training and have an impact on business process re-engineering and internal service management. It was a very different animal to three days earlier. It was bigger, more complex and involved many more stakeholders.

Why had this suddenly all changed? I learned the answer much later on. The CEO was being measured on its success. He then changed Maria's scorecard, making the service quality program worth 50%, instead of the incidental 5% item it had been before.

Suddenly it was a lot more serious and we had to respond accordingly. There was no point pushing the cook-off any further, despite all of the planning we had put into it. It was as dead as the crabs they would have been cooking. A new set of criteria was laid out and we threw out the old program and wrote a new one.

This was not as easy as it may sound and there were many tough moments in redesigning and finally running the workshops. But, eventually, we got there and Maria is a still a client today, although her hair has turned slightly greyer.

So, everything changed when Maria's scorecard changed. She was only interested in achieving those objectives, nothing else. That was her priority. We had to adapt or lose the deal. It was a great lesson in customer behaviour and selling dynamics. Ultimately, it is critical knowledge for negotiating. If I know what *your* most important priority is, I have valuable information to use when negotiating with you. We will come to this a little later in Book 2—Closing the Deal.

Key points

- Your customer's Priority is directly related to their scorecard. Otherwise, why is it their priority?
- Your customer's priority is *your* priority. Change, or go and have a quiet, sullen beer with the other Product-Pushing Snake Oil Salesmen, complaining about your customers.
- The customer's scorecard is what they get measured on. Most big companies have a formal Performance Management System. Every year, at least once, each employee is measured on a list of Key Performance Indicators (KPIs). How well did they go? The final score they get determines whether they:
  a) keep their job or lose it, and / or
  b) get a bonus.

  That's the point.

- *Your* priority as a salesman is to find out what your customer is measured on. If you know your client well, just ask them. In the early stages of a relationship though, you can uncover the main drivers by asking more subtle questions.
- The first three stages of the IMPACT model— Investigate, Map, Prioritise—help you do this.

"Let me tell you buddy, right up front. My clients just want to save money or make money. They see me as the expert. The market maker. They don't want me to waste their time using maps and flipcharts and whiteboards—what planet are you guys on? Stick to your guns. Show me the money my friend. That's what I'm all about!"

CHAPTER 9

Ask the client what they want

Having assisted the client in mapping the process and obstacles and pinpointing their priorities, it is time to start working on a solution. As the salesman, I will naturally be thinking about all of the products and services we have that can meet the need, and how much we will make from this deal. But the golden rule here is to shut up about that and keep asking questions.

Find out what kind of solution the client wants. Many people ask me: "Why bother doing this? We are limited in what we can offer. We can't go customising our products to every client. It would cost too much, reduce profit and take too long."

This is probably true. Not everyone has the luxury of being able to customise solutions around specific client requirements, right?

Wrong! It all depends on how you look at it. Are you trying to sell a product, or fix a customer's problem?

This is the central question in selling.

If I am trying to sell a product, I will concentrate on the features of the product and figure how to position it to meet the customer's need. There's nothing wrong with that, is there?

Yes—it's the wrong way to look at it.

How do you know what your customer really wants as a solution, unless you ask them? By assuming that you know, you are actually hoping your one-size-fits-all solution will do the job. You begin to product-push, which undoes all of your analytical work and raises suspicion levels.

It may appear that all your questions were really just part of a cunning scheme to make the customer feel they were special, but in fact you're just going to offer the same product everyone gets. All roads lead to Rome. There goes the trust in one moment.

It's quite a dilemma, but with a simple solution. Ask the customer what they have in mind and wait with your pen poised. Remember, the most important skill in selling is taking notes, not talking. You can't learn while you are talking. Uncovering interests is impossible if you're a focusing on your own.

Finding a solution

Instead, ask the customer: "If you could imagine this issue being fixed, how would things work? Can you describe what you have in mind?" When the customer starts describing the desired state, write down everything they tell you.

This is what they want to see in your proposal. This is why note-taking is critical. Learn to write fast while maintaining with eye contact. Take off your salesman's hat and picture yourself as a problem-solver.

People are far more likely to respond favourably to something they invented, rather than a standard proposal. Everyone's situation is different, because they are driven by differing incentives. The solution they want will positively impact their incentives, otherwise why would they be proposing it?

Take notes, ask questions, such as "How would that work? Who will benefit from that change? Why? How much?"

And continue to take notes. You will find out exactly what your client wants, and how they want it presented to them.

Don't forget, in most cases there will be multiple layers of decision-making. When your customer is describing their best case scenario for making their life a lot better and you understand exactly what they want, you have everything you need. Write it all down. You may even uncover hidden benefits of your potential solution you may not have thought about before.

Shape your proposal around this. It's much easier for your client to sell the solution internally if they designed it.

Case Study 7: The Financial Planner

My friend, How Nee, is am middle-aged company director. He was telling me about his decision to buy key man insurance. It was a classic play-off between the Product-Pushing Snake Oil Salesman and the Sales Partner—one doing it right and the other doing it all wrong.

How Nee takes every single call he receives from telemarketers. He listens to their pitch. He gets a sheet of paper and takes notes. What does he like about the approach and what doesn't he like? What draws him towards the person and what pushes him away. It's a simple approach and one I have adopted.

He said to me one day: "It's great—I get a free training lesson every time I take the call. Mostly it's 'how not to sell' but sometimes I am genuinely impressed. Like this lady who sold me key man insurance."

He described the scene—taking a call in the evening from one big insurance company, being bombarded with features and benefits, being talked over, interrupted and generally treated obnoxiously (all too typical telephone-selling behaviours). Clearly he had the Snake Oil Salesman on the phone.

He said: "I was actually interested but this lady wouldn't stop talking. She didn't draw a breath. She didn't ask me if I had time to talk, if I had any insurance, if I have any needs in this area. She just rabbited on and on, until I just hung up on her. I couldn't take it any more. I feel sorry for her, but some people are just untrainable. I didn't even want to spend two minutes coaching her, because I knew she would interrupt me. It was awful.

"The next day I took a call from a financial planner. She was the complete opposite. First of all she asked me if I had time to talk and said she only wanted two minutes of my time. Here's how the conversation went."

Financial Planner (Wendy): "Good morning, My name is Wendy Schnapps calling from Bonanza Financial Planning. May I please speak with Mr How Nee Low?"

Customer (How Nee): "Yes that's me, how can I help you?"

Wendy: "Thank you sir, how may I address you?"

How Nee: "How Nee is fine, thank you."

Wendy: "Thank you How Nee, may I have two minutes of your time? I would like to have a quick discussion around financial planning and your needs, if any, in this area. Would that be OK?"

How Nee: "Sure Wendy. What would you like to talk about?"

Wendy: "Thank you. Firstly may I just check with you How Nee, are you still involved in Fook On Construction, as MD?"

How Nee (impressed): "Yes I am Wendy, how did you know that?"

Wendy: "Well I have been taking a look at your company and can see that you are doing well. The recent transaction in getting the Diamond Vale Estate showroom fit-out received a lot of attention. I've actually been to it and it is impressive, professionally finished."

How Nee (really impressed): "Well thanks very much Wendy. What took you there?"

Wendy: "My boyfriend and I are in the market for an investment property and when we went to the showroom, I commented on how good it looks. I saw your name on the prospectus and thought it would be good to talk with you. So I looked you up on LinkedIn, checked out your internet site and, well, thought I should call you. I have several clients with broadly similar professional profiles to yours and would like to understand more about your financial position and plans."

How Nee: "Sorry Wendy, when you say broadly similar, what do you mean?"

Wendy: "Entrepreneurs, early to mid-50s, running the business and involved in day to day operations—selling, designing proposals, running the project, handling customers, getting new deals, balancing lots of things, including finances. Is this the same for you?

How Nee: "Well Wendy, you may as well be describing me. What have you got in mind?"

Wendy: "How Nee, my approach is, with your permission, to analyse in detail your business operations and how that impacts your financial position, now and in the future. But that will take some time, we can't do that in the next 45 seconds. I have already taken your time today, which I really appreciate. Can I arrange another time to talk when you have one hour? I can meet you at your convenience."

How Nee: "That's a good idea Wendy, sure why not? Let's meet next Wednesday at 10 o'clock in my office."

Wendy: "Thank you very much How Nee. In advance of our meeting I want to send you two things: my CV, and a non-disclosure agreement. Please look at the agreement. I will need to collect some personal information from you to assess your situation and possible requirements. Even if we decide there's no immediate opportunity for either of us, you need to be comfortable in sharing information with me. Is your email HNL@FookOnCons.com?"

How Nee smiling "Yes that's right Wendy. You have certainly done your homework. Thank you. See you next week".

How Nee laughed while he told me this story. He said: "I've been selling all my life, and I know a sales pitch when I hear one but this wasn't a sales pitch. She genuinely seemed interested in me.

"Look I know she's probably going to give me an insurance proposal and I expect that, but I was really interested in meeting her. She was different to everyone I've met in this field. I've met a lot of them, mostly Snake Oil Salesmen. They take your money, ignore your needs, invest in high-yield securities and duck for cover when the market collapses, blaming it on everyone and hiding behind the fine print. They're all a bunch of crooks, but she just broke the mould. I arranged to meet her."

"Wow," I said, "that's something, coming from a cynic like you. What happened then?"

"Well I *did* check her out on LinkedIn. Impressive background, *most* professional."

"I get it," I said, "you were going on a date!"

"No, no, nothing like that," he insisted, "she has a boyfriend. This was strictly professional."

"Sure", I said, "OK, get on with it, what happened?"

He then described the meeting conversation.

Wendy: "Thanks very much for meeting me How Nee. How much time do you have today?"

How Nee: "Ninety minutes Wendy, I have another meeting in the city at 12.15. Is that OK?"

Wendy: "Sure, thank you. Before we talk about your situation, I need to advise you of my professional obligations to you . . .

How Nee: "Thanks Wendy, where do we start?"

Wendy: "May I use your whiteboard?"

How Nee (leaning back in his chair): "Of course."

Wendy (picking up the marker): "OK, let's start with the business process. Please talk me through it. How do you go about generating demand and transforming that into profitable business ventures . . ."

"She was good, man, she scared me. She made me realise that unless I did something to protect myself, if I got hit by a bus, the business would come crashing down. And she didn't talk about products or insurance or anything. She just asked questions and drew it all up on the board. Then she asked me, 'What would a great solution look like? Something that would enable you to not worry ever again?'"

"I said to her, 'I thought that was your job!'"

She laughed and said: "My job is to make your life easier. I need to know what that would look like, to you and your family. Then I can figure out a way of helping you achieve that."

"She was brilliant—she made me describe the solution I wanted, how it would work, how much it would cost, what benefits it would bring to everyone—my family, the business. It was really interesting to do this. The funny thing was, she didn't interrupt me at all. She just clarified comments, took notes, asked a few questions and kept writing. I felt like I was in therapy."

"All right," I said, "go on, what happened next?"

How Nee interrupted me: "Sorry man, I've got my other phone ringing. I've gotta go. Talk next week. Sorry, bye!"

Key points

- Do your homework. Show interest in your client's business. Even the most minor reference to the work you've done learning about your client will be met with surprise and gratitude. Why? Because, it means you are focusing on their needs, not yours.
- Speak to people in similar industries to gain insight into the issues your client may face. Ask permission to uncover information. Ask questions. Don't offer solutions until the client asks you what you think.
- Set a time for your phone call or meeting, and stick to it.
- Ask your client what they have in mind. They tend to know what they want, but just can't seem to find it. People tend to be fiercely proud of their own ideas. Why? It's tied to self-esteem. I would like to think that *my* ideas, as the *client,* might be worth *something.* If you fail to overlook this opportunity to build the relationship, you have missed the point.
- Listen, take notes. Write down everything they say. And tell them what they told you. This is the turning point.

"My clients haven't got a clue what they want or need. They depend on me for that advice—that's why I hit 'em up for some serious premiums. They see me as a Thought Leader, a Trusted Financial Advisor. I didn't get there by asking questions. I got there by instilling the fear of God in them, telling them what they need to do and signing them up on the spot. I've even got a mobile credit card machine with me these days. Strike while the iron's hot my man. Don't waste your time asking all these stupid bloody questions."

CHAPTER 10

Confirm understanding

I was intrigued by How Nee's meeting with Wendy, and was keen to hear more. She was following the IMPACT model.

Investigate—do your homework. She knew about How Nee's business, certainly enough to impress him initially.

Map—analyse the business processes and look for strengths, weaknesses, opportunities, threats. She found out that he was the principal breadwinner, architect, project manager and service officer. There were several holes in that model.

Prioritise—his priority was to cover his family in case of serious injury, so the cash flow would not be affected.

Ask—about a good solution. He explained all of the things he wanted in place to make him feel more at ease. Wendy simply asked questions, listened, clarified and took notes.

Now it was time for Wendy to address the final two parts of the IMPACT formula: Confirm understanding and Tailoring a solution.

So what happened next? How did Wendy close a key man insurance deal with someone who thought he had all the bases covered? There's a ton of companies out there selling insurance. What was her point of difference?

Let's look at what she didn't do. She didn't blurt out a solution. She kept asking questions and clarifying. Going back to the conversation . . .

Case Study 7: The Financial Planner (cont.)

How Nee: "Wendy I can see now that there is a big cash flow risk I am carrying and a lot of downside if something happens to me. What do you propose I should do?"

Wendy: "There's several things we will do from here and then you can decide what to do. Firstly, I'm going to summarise everything you just told me. Here and now. Secondly, I am going to write a report that I will send to you, confirming the details. Thirdly, I need you to validate the information. In the meantime I will work on some potential strategies for mitigating that risk. My objective is to get you a comprehensive solution at minimal cost. Then I can send you a proposal, and come over and clarify it with you. Does that sound OK?"

How Nee (super impressed): "Absolutely, please go ahead."

Wendy: "OK, thanks How Nee. What I understand is as follows: 75% of your business comes from referrals, 20% through direct sales effort, and 5% through the internet . . .

. . . .

How Nee rang me a few days later. "Sorry Bern, I got stuck on a few things."

83

"Lucky I wasn't holding my breath mate."

"Anyway, all jokes aside, she was great, determined to get it right—every single detail. She was systematic, explaining our business back to me and showing where the vulnerabilities lay. She quantified the risks at each point and said to me: 'You have to work out which of these you are prepared to live with and which ones you need to cover. I can help you in that assessment. Most importantly, I need to leave the room today with you confident that I understand your total position. Because only then can we work on some strategies. How confident are you, How Nee?'"

"I told her she was bang on the money. When she left the office I felt a renewed sense of confidence in the future. I felt a weight lifted off my shoulder. I felt good about the world. I was really impressed with Wendy and she hadn't mentioned any solutions, pricing—nothing! She was really like a therapist doing the first meeting with the new patient.

"I already sensed she was right—the right person we needed to advise us on the business and our risk management. And, I had only met her for an hour and she had not presented one single idea. She was interested in me and only me. It was revolutionary, especially for that industry of Product-Pushing Snake Oil Salesmen. I couldn't wait to see her report.

"So the report is emailed to me within four hours. Again, this was way outside of my expectations. I thought she'd either forget or at least take a few days. She rang me to make sure I received it and asked me to call her when I was ready to talk again. 'Please review the details thoroughly—I don't want to have any misunderstandings'. I felt like a schoolboy, but was enjoying the process and discipline."

"OK, how was the report? Did she get it right?"

"It was perfect—only a couple of minor points. She delivered the goods. I rang her to tell her how impressed I was with her work and that I was keen to get the proposal."

"The proposal came back within two days. For ten grand a year, US, I was covered to my eyeballs, provided I pass the medical. Wendy came around to discuss it with me, on time, as usual, all business. Then she did something really unusual."

"Oh, ho, ho, what was that?" I asked, my eyes rolling and my mind wandering. "Did she give you another proposal?"

"Well, I'm joking, I just wanted to hear your reaction. I wanted to see the substance before spending that sort of money. But she didn't pitch the proposal to me. She made me present it back to her. As if I was selling the deal to her! It was outrageous. I said to her, not for the first time, 'Isn't this your job? Aren't you supposed to be selling to me?'

"She said: 'I'm not selling anything How Nee. All I want to know is does this make sense? It's your life, not mine. I want you to be sure this proposal is right for you, not me. And, if you like it, you may have to convince others, such as your wife. You need to believe every aspect, every number in that proposal, before you go down that path. Let's set up another time, in two days, so you can present it to me. I will pretend to be the people you need to influence—your business partners'."

"She really did that?" I asked, genuinely surprised. I had never heard of any insurance salesperson doing this before. Normally they just push and push until you tell them to just go away. But it almost seemed How Nee had to earn the right to do business with Wendy. She wanted her clients to understand everything they were getting into, the merits of the proposal, before they signed anything.

So he did it. He formally presented the proposal to Wendy, as if he was presenting to his wife and management team. She brought two of her colleagues along to play the part. They asked difficult questions and didn't allow him to skip over them. They posted all the questions he couldn't answer on a chart and went through them in detail with him. They raised objections about the proposal—the need, the cost, the benefit, the alternatives, had he thought about this, had he thought about that?

Then he had to do it again in 10 minutes—the challenge faced and the solution proposed. Again he was grilled like a star witness at a Hollywood celebrity trial. At the end, after he survived, and when they were sure their man was ready to sell the product to the other decision-makers, Wendy asked him, "Any questions?".

Looking exhausted, How Nee said: "Only one. But let me sign this acceptance letter now. It's a done deal. Here's the first cheque, already signed by the finance guy. He's been nagging me to do something about this for years. I just wanted to see how good you were."

Wendy was up on her feet. "Are you sure?", she asked uncertainly.

"Absolutely," How Nee said, genuinely taken aback by Wendy's sincerity, her desire to do the right thing by her clients.

"Well there is cooling down period," she hastened to add. "This will be valid from today for 30 days, upon signature. But before you sign, you said you had one more question. Please, what is it?"

"I'm joking," said How Nee, laughing "I just wanted to see if you picked that up, or if you were desperate to get me to sign. You passed every test. You are brilliant. Congratulations on a great job."

"Well thank you How Nee, and welcome to Bonanza. I will be your personal manager. Anything you need, at all, I will attend to. Tomorrow I will call you to go through our service agreement, and to ask if there are any issues you would like to discuss. Thank you for your business. It's a privilege to deal with you."

. . . .

How Nee was having fun telling me this story. There was a fabulous sales message in it.

"Look it's a great story How Nee," I said to him over a drink one evening at our regular haunt, "but let's face it—it's only an insurance deal. There must be more to this. Why are you so effusive about this Wendy? She sounds fantastic but, I have to ask, was there any underlying motivation to do this deal with her?"

At that moment a waitress materialised with a bottle of Verve Cliquot and four glasses. Surprised by the gesture from the red wine connoisseur How Nee, and upon seeing the third and fourth glasses, I looked up curiously at the waitress, a Caucasian women, unusual in this role in Singapore. She smiled at me and filled my glass.

Then How Nee's wife, Pia, a glamorous Swedish heart surgeon, sauntered up to our table and pecked us both on the cheek. "Good evening gentlemen, I hope I haven't interrupted anything. Looks like trouble, you two together in a pub."

"Hmm", I thought, an announcement of some kind. It's not often that Pia descends into the dubious surrounds of the bars where How Nee and others of our kind congregate.

Then, the waitress sat down at our table and poured the rest of the champagne. Most unusual, I thought. How Nee and Pia sat there in amusement watching me struggle with the unfolding events. Pia took a sip of her champagne and decided to put me out of my misery.

"Bern, meet Wendy Schnapps, our new head of sales."

Key points

- Take your time. Don't try to close the deal too early. Make sure you understand everything possible about your client and their business. Confirm you understand by telling them the story.
- Make the best use of your client's time. Check how much time they have and stick to it.
- Objections are natural. Clients usually express these by saying things like "But, what would happen if . . . ?" or "Well, I'm not really sure if we need to do this". Listen to everything your client says, write it down and then clarify it. Don't feel compelled to respond there and then. Deals of any real value take some time and usually need several people to agree.
- Think of yourself as a joint problem-solver. People will trust you more if they perceive you are interested in their needs rather than your own. Building trust takes time and effort.

*The offer closes at
5 o'clock - let's shake on it now,
you don't want to
miss out*

"Sure! Great story! It's a happy ending, but unlikely. She's got all her eggs in the one basket and playing with fire. How much time did she spend on this guy? What happens if he blows her out? How many other deals are in her pipeline? You can't do business like this and expect it to work every time? Slippery road that one. She won't last a year in Sales."

CHAPTER 11

Tailoring a solution

So Wendy was the real deal. She did everything right. She was so good her customer hired her. Of course there are many Wendy stories, where people are so impressed with the person selling to them that they hire them. But what is the point of difference?

Is there an element of magic in this lottery of whether someone buys from you? Whether they recommend you, hire you, or buy your company?

In my view there is. It is all about the action you take at this stage of the game. You are almost there; the customer is asking you for a proposal. Why? Because their priorities are now aligned with yours—they need what you have to offer, and now.

Now the fun starts. Getting the business. Welcome to the minefield of subtleties and unexploded devices just waiting to be part of *that* action. After all this hard work in using the IMPACT model, realistically, all you have done is get one or two people interested in what you have to offer. It's better than no-one being interested! But it's just the beginning—albeit a great beginning.

You have created an internal sales force—someone who wants the change and is willing to push it, because it will positively impact their scorecard. Assuming there are no competitors, they *need* you.

But that is a big assumption. Competitors exist everywhere. There are two kinds: inside the client organisation and outside. But we are getting ahead of ourselves here—let's cover the final steps in ***Opening the Deal.***

Prepare the report

There are several critical stages in Tailoring the solution. We have left the client meeting, having confirmed understanding to their satisfaction and they are now eagerly awaiting the report.

1. Write the report within 24 hours. Factually, concisely. Give it to your colleagues to check grammar, spelling and construction. Send it to your client as a draft. See Appendix 1: Sample Call Report, Set follow-up actions.
2. Send an email or call the customer to make sure they have received the report. Ask if they have any questions or if there are errors.
3. Change the details accordingly and ask for permission to send a proposal.
4. Ask your client when they would like to see a proposal, who will be looking at it and how much detail should it involve. How will the proposal be evaluated?
5. Ask about the profile and styles of the people reviewing the proposal. What are their KPIs? What are they likely to be interested in? Who are the potential detractors? Why? What do they want? Take a lot of notes.

Develop the solution

Case Study: The Doberman with Lipstick

I once worked in sales in a bank in Asia, let's call them Oriental Bank. In my first three months, a senior vice-president said to me: "We're meeting ABC Corporation next week, can you present a regional cash management solution to them? They are a very important client."

I asked: "What are their problems?"

She said, dismissively: "The same as everyone's. They all have the same issues in Asia, trying to manage their cash in 20 countries, complicated with confusing financial regulations. Just give them the same presentation you gave XYZ last week—it covers the key points. But make sure you don't talk about regional funds pooling— we will lose a lot of revenue if we introduce them to that concept."

I was pretty new in Asia, and I was dealing with an "old Asia hand". This person managed all of the Multinational Corporation relationships at the bank. She was feared by her colleagues, not to be messed with—a "Doberman with Lipstick". I did what I was told and regurgitated the old presentation at the meeting.

The client we were presenting to was generating more than USD5 million a year for our bank. In anyone's eyes, this is a great client. One you want to protect, look after and bring new ideas to help them become more profitable. Build the trust.

One million of this revenue was made up of the interest the bank earned on the money left in ABC's accounts every night. We paid next to nothing in interest to our client. We loaned out their balances overnight on the money market at around 10 per cent. It was, as they say in the trade, a "nice little earner".

The client was painfully aware of this and had respectfully asked us, as their global banker, to help them become more efficient with the use of this money. After all, they were borrowing money in China and had excess funds in the Middle East they didn't know about and could have used. It was like borrowing 20 grand from your bank to buy a new car and realising afterwards you had the money in another account. The only problem was your 20 grand loan required interest payments when you could have used your own funds. It all costs money and it all adds up.

Our banking systems didn't allow ABC to know how much cash they had in the bank across all their countries of operation, or enable them to use it. This cost them a ton of money. On the other hand, it made *us* a lot of money, on the interest income.

The client had a huge financial incentive to change. We had an equal incentive to not change anything.

Or, I should say, the head of client relationships had a lot to lose. She was measured on revenue to the bank. If we introduced a new system for helping the client better manage their balances, we would lose around 300 grand in revenue on this client alone. This would impact the Doberman's performance that year and reduce her bonus. Plus, she was retiring next year. She had zero incentive to help the client, despite her illustrious title as head of client relationships.

She decided the best "solution" was to keep things the way they were. Make it sound really difficult to change things. Regulations, new systems, new procedures—all too hard. Understandably, the client was discouraged. Equally understandably, the client advised us four weeks later they were moving all of their business to Bank AAA, who demonstrated how they could save the client 600 grand a year.

What did the Doberman do? She made it even more difficult for the client. Refused exceptions on credit lines. Tightened policy around payment instructions, everything she could think of to keep the revenue coming in until she retired. Why? She was looking after her own interests and not the client's. Twenty years later, ABC does not do any substantial business with Oriental. They don't trust them and everyone knows why.

Epilogue

The Doberman retired and strolled off into the sunset with her bonus, hand-in-hand with the Product-Pushing Snake Oil Salesman, leaving the carnage in her wake. They made a lovely couple.

Main Points

1. Help the client. Not yourself.
2. A solution is rarely a standard product. It is a dedicated approach to resolving client problems.
3. Solutions fix client problems—they don't add to them.
4. Think from the client's perspective, not your own.

I'm not saying you pillage your revenue streams to give love to the client. Don't give away the shop. Negotiate. Help them find savings and offer these savings contingent upon future business.

This is fair and reasonable. But be aware of this reality of business: if you are making a ton of money out of a client, they will be aware of it and will want to reduce the expense. If they highlight this and you refuse to change things, you are a Product-Pushing Snake Oil Salesman. And when they fire you, they won't shake your hand. They'll kick your arse *that* hard you'll be having nose-bleeds. Your reputation will be shattered. And unhappy customers have a nasty habit of reappearing in your life, just at the wrong time.

And that puts the final nail in the Snake Oil Salesman's coffin.

So avoid this behaviour. Be professional. Help your client. They will remember you for all the right reasons.

Here's a better approach:

1. Share the validated call report with your colleagues, and other parties critical to the deal.
2. Brainstorm options. How can we give them something better than what they have now? What capabilities do we have now and what development work must we do? How much will this cost, how long will it take and who's paying for it?
3. Agree all costs in advance and get consensus to proceed.
4. Write the DRAFT proposal. 2-5 pages, focus on customer needs, the solution and how it solves the problems. Speak the customer's language. Don't bullshit on about your company. Quantify. Demonstrate value—the cost of implementing the proposal versus the benefits achievable. Be conservative. Include a roll-out schedule (see Appendix 2: Sample proposal & business writing techniques).
5. Share the proposal with your colleagues. Gain their agreement to commitments made, pricing, wording and implementation schedules.

6. Once agreed by all key stakeholders, double and triple-check the spelling and grammar. Cut out all unnecessary information. Avoid making glowing statements about how good you are—focus on the client and their needs.

7. Send it to your client as a DRAFT.

8. Get informal feedback. "What are your first thoughts on the proposal? Who is likely to support the proposal, and vice versa? For the detractors, what do they want?" Take detailed notes. Be prepared to rewrite the document several times.

9. Submit the new version and set a follow-up date within one week. Send an agenda for the meeting (see Appendix 3: Sample meeting agenda).

10. Confirm the meeting and who will be there. Look them all up on LinkedIn. Look at who they are connected to. Get in touch with common connections. Ask them what they know about the people you are meeting. Are they analytical types, sociable, serious or quick decision-makers? You must know this so you can prepare and have a message for each style. You must be able to speak their language.

11. For each style, have a plan:
    a. Analytical: your approach must be factual, logical, well structured, based on evidence and research
    b. Sociable: informality, lighten the mood with humour, show flexibility and willingness to compromise
    c. Serious: the proposal discussion must focus on quality and benefits, fitting into company values and complying with strict standards
    d. Quick-decision makers: get to the point quickly, using numbers to prove your point. Be confident. Speak in short sentences

12. If the client asks you to do a presentation, clarify the objective. Be crystal clear. Arrange your content around it—

what must they know, need to know and what is nice to know. Be prepared to leave out the latter.

13. Keep presentations short and powerful. They must have a hook in the first 10 seconds to grab people's attention.

14. Prepare the presentation and send three days in advance to your sponsor, the person who wants to see the change. Check it through thoroughly with them. Ask about sensitivities. Be sharp on cultural / political / business issues. Get up to date info—did the company just buy another business? Are they shedding staff? You must know this—if you don't, your proposal may be shredded, along with you, in the first five minutes.

15. Ask your contact to arrange a room with a whiteboard or flipchart—bring your own pens. Make sure they are erasable.

16. Practise working with flipcharts and whiteboards. These are your friends in the meeting room. You control the meeting. You change the game when you use these invaluable tools (see Appendix 4: Whiteboards and flipcharts).

17. Turn up early for the meeting, making sure everything is in place—projectors working, enough materials for everyone. Repeat the IMPACT process in your presentation. Deliver the hook. Use numbers if available and provable. Spend the next five minutes finding out who's there and what they are interested in. Capture the comments in full view of the group. Use this as a resource for the meeting. Focus entirely on these interests, and connect them to your proposal.

18. Ask for feedback and take notes. Repeat the feedback without getting defensive. Say what you will do about it, and by when. Then repeat the whole process until you get agreement. Rome wasn't built in a day

If you've got this far, you're on the right track. GOOD LUCK! Many more tips on presentations, negotiations and relationship management in Book 2, Closing the Deal.

Key points

- Almost every salesperson / account / relationship manager talks to their clients about "solutions". Solutions are means of solving a problem or dealing with a difficult situation.
- Solutions are the correct answer to a puzzle. Understand the puzzle before blurting out "solutions". It sounds good in theory, but it's challenging to resist doing this, especially when you know your product is so good.
- Be prepared to work hard, change your thinking, ask questions and wait. Your customers' priorities will change, and if you're not prepared to, enlist in the Snake Oil Salesman's alumni—a group of bitter and twisted shysters who drink their beers and pine for the Good Old Days.

The Doberman With Lipstick

The Snake Oil Salesman's view

"Look I don't meant to be cynical, but you're missing the main point. All this talk about addressing customers' needs is fine if you've got time, which I don't. I've got customers to sell to. Building new 'solutions' for every whim of the customer costs money, and let me tell you, these bastards are out to get you. The moment you start cutting costs and eating into your own money, they won't let up. Give them an inch and they'll take a mile. Look after yourself Bud, no-one else is going to.

But, if you believe all of this crap in this book, it's time to start working for the United Nations. Or become a primary school teacher, or something. Good luck, Mother Teresa!"

CHAPTER 12

Short-Term, Long-Term Relationship

The temptation of the juicy short-term deal is well recognised. Especially if you haven't done a deal for a while. But customers are not stupid. They usually have a few options to choose from, and a pretty good idea of how much they are prepared to pay to fix the problem. Be fair in your dealings, putting yourself in the customers' shoes as much as you can.

Case Study 10: The Forgetful Client

We agreed in principle a consulting rate for a three-month project in China. I agreed to take off 5% if we received a commitment in writing for the deal. We all shook hands and went to dinner, excited about working together. There were lots of Xing Tao beers, the mandatory bottles of whiskey, and the inevitable KTV lounge for drunken middle-aged men to collapse hysterically to their knees, wailing indecipherable Chinese love songs. Life-long friendships formed.

Pretty normal night, really, in Asia.

The next day the contract arrived by email. All the details were right, including the commitment on the new project, with an even longer engagement period than I expected, and all at the same daily rate. Fantastic! But they had forgotten to include the 5% discount I had agreed. This amounted to about USD 25,000.

"Wow! 25 grand for free!" exclaimed the Snake Oil Salesman excitedly. "About time we got one up on the bastards. They've always been trying to rip us off, screwing us on the price. Let's just sign the contract and send it back to them. Then it's done. Great, rebook the holiday to California! Business Class."

But the Sales Partner took a dim view of this short-term thinking. He tapped the Snake Oil Salesman on the shoulder and whispered in his ear:

"Don't be such an idiot! They are testing you. They want to know if they can trust you. If you sign that document and send it back, they will find a way out of the contract and never do business with you again. This company has been in business for 100 years— they don't want to deal with short-term opportunists. Highlight the mistakes, and send back what you believe are the agreed terms. That 25 grand, which you will never see anyway, is nothing compared to the reputation and future business you will gain by being a fair partner, and pointing out mistakes. They will respect your honesty, and you will never look back."

The Snake Oil Salesman put up a fight. "Look its OK for you. You've made your target. But I'm struggling and this 25 grand will get me the bonus I need to take family on a promised holiday. I say we just play dumb and send it back. They've got so much money, they won't notice. I think we give it a shot! Who dares, wins!"

The Sales Partner isn't impressed. He persists. "After all we've been through in this book, you haven't learned a thing. Every salesperson is given a short-term sales target, and I know this is sometimes difficult to reach. It's a target, not a relationship, and it's a shame you're not measured on the latter. But right now, it's your choice. Short-term gain often equals long term pain. Your career is determined by your reputation. People you are meeting now can have an uncomfortable knack of turning up again in your life, when you least expect it. If you take advantage of an honest mistake now they will remember you as the petty thief you are, forever, and spreading that news just got a whole lot easier with social media.

Tell them they made a mistake. Show them you are to be trusted. Do this all the time. Be fair and reasonable. Work together. Treat your customers the way you would like to be treated. Don't be some scum-of-the-earth salesman all of your life! Take Ten Minutes Off and be Honest! You will be that far in front, you'll be lonely!

'The Snake Oil Salesman corking up another deal'

CHAPTER 13

Conclusion

Selling, as in being a Sales Partner, is a tough game. Not many people want a job where you are constantly on the hook to bring in revenue. It's non-stop; it consumes you. Hopefully this book gives you some logical steps to make the best use of your time. Spray & Pray is inefficient.

The IMPACT model helps you focus on the clients who *want* to work with you, who are definitely looking to improve things. Wouldn't it be better to spend your valuable time with these people, rather than those who aren't interested and can't wait to get away from you?

We all sell, whether it be trying to win a case, or a deal, or presenting a project plan, writing an email, convincing your kids to go to school camp, or applying for a new job. Our lives are largely about convincing people to do things—read something, learn something, do something, don't do something. Unless you understand that people are driven by their own incentives, not yours, you will be doing a lot of Spraying and a hell of a lot more Praying.

Is the Product-Pushing Snake Oil Salesman really dead?

No, of course not. There will always be plenty of them around. But in the world of global business and long-term relationships, there is no place for this style. Once people realise his intent is not genuine, that he really only cares about himself, he will be spurned like a rabid dog. This is not good for his career.

The Golden Rule: Life is not easy. You're dead for a long time, be good to everyone. They'll remember you for the right reasons.

Appendix 1: Sample call report

Appendix 2: Sample proposal & business writing techniques

Appendix 3: Sample meeting agenda

Appendix 4: Whiteboards and flipcharts

Appendix 1: Sample Call Report

Rationale: Call Reports record what happened in the meeting. They should be written within 24 hours, otherwise it is so easy to forget the main points and the subtleties of the discussion. It's useful to follow the IMPACT Model, so you build up the case for action.

They don't have to be complicated, just 1-2 pages of notes in a logical format will do. Once you've finished it, give it to a colleague to read. Correct spelling and grammar mistakes. Send it to the client as a record, asking them for input. 99% of the time they won't respond, but they will be impressed with your attention to detail. It creates a great first impression. Including Next Steps (with dates) at the foot of the report enables you to set the agenda for the next meeting.

CALL REPORT

COMPANY:	FRONTIER Singapore Pte Ltd
DATE:	January 24, 2014
FROM SOP:	May Lee Chung, Head of HR
FROM IMPACT:	Bernie Jones
PURPOSE:	Discuss Implementation of the Performance Management Programme

Investigation

There are four functional companies under the Frontier umbrella, each with their own corporate objectives and business plans:

- Frontier Rigs
- Frontier Audit

- Frontier Subsea
- Frontier Logistics

There are approximately 570 Singapore-based employees, 65% of whom are Singaporean and 35% foreigners.

There is a strategic HR initiative introducing the Lominger competency framework. This framework has been adopted to determine four specific role functions for which there are generic competency needs. These are Individual Contributor, Team Leader, Operational Leader and Strategic Leader. All roles in the group have been allocated into one of these functional descriptions. At the same time The Performance Development System is migrating to an electronic platform.

In June / July HR presented the strategy through many workshops. All staff were trained to write their job objectives so they are aligned with SMART principles, corporate objectives and values.

Mapping

The new approach represented a major change from the traditional top down, paper-based system of the past, and several challenges arose in implementing this strategy. The major issue was gaining company-wide acceptance of and commitment to the new processes (of writing their own objectives) in time for the 2013 Performance Reviews. Frontier encountered a lot of resistance—people were too busy, didn't see the point of the exercise, didn't see it as important, it was too difficult, and a lot of work that wasn't their job.

There were questions around reward systems, feasibility and sustainability of this approach. Despite many reminders and pushing from HR the result was poor-quality objectives and ambiguity over quantifiable elements.

Priority

The Performance Review process encountered numerous problems with people being dissatisfied with the outcomes. Ratings and accompanying remuneration decisions were unacceptable to many people, causing internal repercussions. The priority is to rewrite all Performance Objectives in time for the March HR launch. Failure to do so will create backlashes and potential resignations.

Actions Required

The company is continuing with the system and is looking for help refining the previous work to enhance the level of acceptance. Frontier has asked IMPACT for a proposal as to how we would drive the required change through a series of training workshops. There is a sense of urgency in completing this by mid-March 2014.

January 26: IMPACT to submit proposal
January 28: Meeting with Frontier to discuss the proposal

Appendix 2: Sample Proposal and Business Writing Techniques

Q. What does this mean?

Over the past few years we have experienced a significant growth in various businesses through new product offerings requiring substantial systems developments and change requests. The broader financial information and technology infrastructure has not kept pace with business growth and complexity, resulting in sub optimal information flow between operating and processing systems. Audit has a critical role to play here in ensuring that all documentation is in place, the financials are in place, the reporting and approval processes are clearly documented and in accordance with company policy, and all of the key processes are in place. Notwithstanding this the investment in the systems enhancements with respect to financial and accounting information has been minimal in comparison to the magnitude of business growth—Audit now has an opportunity to play an active role in defining operational processing data requirements and standards. This phase of the project is a remediation of issues which over time has been plaguing the audit function resulting in manual journals / manual workarounds to circumvent the inefficiencies in the operating systems. The key objective of the Z2Q Systems Enhancement Project will be to get these issues addressed and drive an environment of transactional activity is ubiquitous, unbounded by traditional constraints associated with manual processes and tactical workarounds. The associated impact on account of these amendments and permanent enhancements to downstream systems has been duly considered at a strategic level. These process improvements are aligned with our continuous improvement objectives and harmonised business conditions for creating a best-in-class control risk environment by automating processes and reducing and/or eliminating manual workarounds. This initiative, in addition to addressing finance issues, also encompasses some of the other bank-wide operations related issues which are currently managed by group Audit in conjunctions with the 2020 SBIs. Specifically the realignment . . . .

A. Who knows?

What they should have said

The objective of this project is to:

- Improve the speed and accuracy of information flowing between XYZ systems
- Reduce Regulatory and Operational Risks

People in business generally write poorly. They use big words to impress the reader. They write long sentences that leave the reader suffocating. They bury the facts and actions so deeply the reader doesn't know what they are talking about. They usually make spelling and grammatical mistakes, thinking it is OK. And they wonder why they didn't get anywhere.

Writing succinctly is a non-negotiable in selling. A great tip is

1. Tell them what you are going to tell them—Hook and Introduction
2. Tell them a logical argument—Body of the document
3. Tell them what you told them—Summary and Conclusion

Use numbers—they are far more convincing than words. But you must be able to back them up.

There are many books on proposal writing. I do like *Sales Proposals for Dummies*—Bob Kantin, and *Persuasive Business Proposals*—Tom Sant. Websites obviously abound as well.

Here is a summary of the critical elements of a proposal:

1. Simple stuff—Introduction—Body—Conclusion / Summary.
2. Hook the reader in the opening line—use numbers "Oriental will increase revenue by 20% by implementing the recommendations of this proposal".
3. Present the client's objective—why they need the proposal.
4. Succinct writing. Short sentences. Simple words.
5. If it is more than four pages long, include an Executive Summary.
6. Avoid jargon and buzzwords, unless they are used by the client (e.g. Client-centricity—see below).
7. State your expertise. Back it up with client testimonials. Ensure clients are willing to put their name to the statement, otherwise it means nothing.
8. Ask your clients to be contactable for verbal references. You'll be surprised how many people actually check you out.
9. Logical structure—use the IMPACT model to build the case.
10. Distinguish between Features (What you are proposing) and Benefits (How it will help the client).
11. Quantify benefits where possible, but be conservative.
12. Break the document into clear, easy to read segments. Use headings and bullet points, but include some conversational sentences as well. Otherwise it looks like it was created by a computer.
13. Include a proposed Implementation Schedule—it shows you are committed to the deal.
14. Be clear about the Investment required (currency). What is included and not included. Travel/ accommodation etc

should be excluded as they can vary quickly with exchange rates. No one likes surprise add-on costs.

The importance of concise, clear business writing.

In business proposal writing, the most common problems are:

- excessive length
- vendor rather than customer focus
- lack of structured argument
- no clear point
- meaningless statements
- industry jargon
- no differentiation between other competing proposals, and
- poor spelling and grammar

A decision-maker will probably distrust a vendor who can't take the time and care to submit a well organised, client-focused, error-free document. What more significant mistakes could happen if the proposal is approved?

In Book 2 "Closing the Deal" we explain how to write documents that achieve their objective. While you wait for that, here is an example of a Proposal. There's no RIGHT WAY, but plenty of wrong ways. Follow these guidelines and you are on the right track.

SAMPLE PROPOSAL

IMPACT Corporate Training Pte. Ltd
9 Raffles Place, Level 58, Republic Plaza
SINGAPORE 048619
Tel: 65—6823 1264, Fax: 65 63441449
Email: berniejones@impactcorporatetraining.com
www.impactcorporatetraining.com

January 31, 2013

Mr. James Ng
Head of Client Experience
Consumer Bank Operations
Oriental Bank
SINGAPORE

Dear James

Consumer Operations Customer-Centricity Project Proposal

IMPACT Corporate Training will be able to help Oriental Bank deliver USD 1.5 million in savings in 2013 by implementing this proposal. The savings will grow to USD 2.2 million in 2014, with IMPACT as your training partner.

Consumer Operations is running a global project to improve its customer service. Your objective is to reduce costs and improve service ratings by 15% in 2013, and 20% in 2014. You need expertise to help you design and execute this project.

IMPACT Corporate Training is an expert in customer service improvement strategies. In this proposal we outline our approach

Bernard J. Jones

to working with Oriental to deliver your goals. We have analysed your savings projections and believe they are achievable, provided there is systematic, automated way of collecting data. We can provide that.

We have clients who will testify to the economic value we create. In our recent Service Excellence project with Bonanza Insurance the return on investment was agreed to be in excess of 500%.

Your project objective is to instill client-centricity into the DNA of Consumer Operations. The services and systems we propose are proven in this field. They are applicable throughout the world and once implemented will have continuous positive outcomes.

I will call you on the 2nd of February to discuss the next steps.

Yours sincerely
Bernie Jones
Managing Director

65-9754 9451
berniejones@impactcorporatetraining.com

(Header—Client Logo and name of Project "Oriental Bank Consumer Operations Client Centricity Project"

Proposal by IMPACT Corporate Training

---

1. Proposed Role for IMPACT

We see IMPACT's role as leading and being involved in the following critical functions:

1. Service consulting and coaching work in launching and sustaining the project
2. Delivering capabilities to drive the project
3. Administration

1.1 Service Consulting & Coaching

IMPACT will provide a Service Coach to advise on the design and execution of the customer-centricity project. Our work will include preparing communications, sharing market information, participating in stakeholder meetings, assisting with project information gathering and reporting, and providing service coaching.

Benefits to Oriental Bank: Customer Service is a key strength of our business. We have global consulting and training experience with satisfied clients and proven, innovative techniques to share with you.

1.2 Delivery Capabilities

We will provide Oriental with our proprietary tools to drive this project. These include the:

- IMPACT Service Behaviours Assessment and Feedback Method ©
- IMPACT Customer-Centricity Survey System ©
- IMPACT Service Behaviours Tactics Guide ©
- IMPACT Service Behaviours Training Modules ©

See Appendix 1 for a brief description of each of these tools.

Intellectual Property Copyright.

All the processes and information are proprietary, confidential, and all rights in the works are reserved.

We have demonstrated these capabilities to the project team and agree our approach is directly applicable to the project goals.

Benefits to Oriental:

- Our IMPACT Service Behaviours Assessment and Feedback Method gives a unique perspective on how to improve customer service by living the Bank's values.
- The Customer-Centricity Survey System provides data to quickly and easily identify strengths and vulnerabilities in service behaviours, and pinpoint areas for improvement.
- The data will be used to formally assess individual and business unit performance.
- The Tactics Guide and Training Modules build skills and knowledge directly applicable to the desired service behaviours.

By implementing these tools all business units will be able to focus on specific service behaviour improvement. They will be able to observe positive changes in their customer satisfaction ratings.

Management can use the data to identify best practices across Consumer Operations and share these through various media. Management will have quantified information to assess performance against corporate values. The information will enable Consumer Operations to confidently report improvements in service perceptions to the key stakeholders.

1.3 Administration

We have developed the software and administration capabilities to support the proposed approach through independent reporting and analysis.

Benefits to Oriental

- Oriental will not have to commit resources to the feedback process
- Oriental will be comfortable with the integrity of the data. Being an external entity with no vested interest in the actual scores and feedback, IMPACT will provide unbiased information and perspectives. An external survey system encourages honest and accurate feedback, and the data is sheltered from unauthorized scrutiny and use.

2. Proposed Engagement Terms

2.1 Service Coaching & Consulting

Our professional fee is USD 0000 per day. This is our agreed daily training delivery rate for Oriental engagements. It does not cover variable costs such as travel, accommodation, and other pre-approved expenses.

Bernard J. Jones

2.2 Delivery Capabilities

IMPACT will license Oriental to use our proprietary materials:

- IMPACT Service Behaviours Assessment and Feedback Method
- IMPACT Customer-Centricity Survey System
- IMPACT Service Behaviours Tactics Guide
- IMPACT Service Behaviours Training Modules

2.3 Survey Administration

IMPACT will administer the Customer-Centricity Survey System at a fee of USD 0000 per month for the first 12 months.

The license fee will be USD 000,000 for the first year. This is payable upon signing an engagement agreement. Other fees will be invoiced monthly and reviewed after 12 months. We await your feedback on the proposal and look forward to working with you to successfully deliver this project.

Investment Summary 2013 (USD)

License   000,000
Advisory   00,000
Administration   00,000

Total   000,000*

* Excluding variable costs (Section 2.1)

3. Summary

Client Service training is our forte. We know we can help Oriental deliver the financial benefits of this project, because we have done it before. We are recognised within the Financial Services sector as a world-class training provider. IMPACT helps its clients save and make money. They are willing to share their experience.

Attachment 1: DELIVERY CAPABILITY TOOLS

> **IMPACT Service Behaviours Assessment and Feedback Method**
>
> Our method gives a unique perspective on how to improve customer service while living the Bank's values. IMPACT created the concept of breaking the values down into observable service behaviours, so staff can understand what is expected of them. Presenting the values in this way it helps people apply the desired behaviours at work.
>
> The IMPACT method enables Consumer Operations to evaluate the extent to which the service behaviours are embraced. We explained this unique methodology to Consumer Operations and produced examples of Service Behaviours relevant to the Bank's values. The project team used this information to develop behaviours applicable to Oriental's values.

IMPACT Client Centricity Survey System

The survey software was developed by IMPACT as an electronic vehicle for obtaining data about the importance and application of the Service Behaviours. Business units invite their own staff (Self Rating) and customers (Customer Rating) to provide numerical ratings on the Importance and Performance of the unit in relation to each Service Behaviour. There is also provision for written comments to help the unit improve its service.

The respondents are directed to a link. Once the linked is opened the Survey is activated. Respondents complete and submit the Survey. The ratings are calculated and averaged, and written responses collated. All information is presented in a 2-page report to the unit head.

The recipient can quickly identify strengths and weaknesses in service behaviours, and pinpoint areas for improvement.

IMPACT Service Behaviour Tactics Guide

For each Service Behaviour there is a corresponding set of tactics to employ to immediately improve performance. These are practical, proven actions that people can take to apply the Service Behaviours and "live the values". The Tactics Guide can be disseminated through the Bank's broadcast system.

IMPACT Service Behaviour Training Modules

IMPACT will design eight Training Modules to be conducted by business unit heads to improve service performance. There will be an Introduction Tutorial, followed by Modules specific to the Values and Service Behaviours. The Training Modules will include facilitation guidelines, exercises, presentation materials, and related visual aids and learning tools.

Attachment 2: About IMPACT Corporate Training

Founded in Singapore in 2001, IMPACT has established itself as a training company renowned for its original and high-impact training programmes. In the Financial Services industry IMPACT has been engaged by Oriental Bank and Bonanza Insurance, to design and deliver a wide range of training programmes. Amongst its MNC client base IMPACT counts Concorde. We have designed and conducted a multitude of technical and behavioural programmes in Australia, Asia, India, the Middle East, South Africa, Europe, the UK, South America and the US.

Client Profile

Company	Industry	Nature of Assignment	Location of Engagement
Oriental Bank	Financial Services	Sales, service, leadership and project management training	Europe, USA
Bonanza Insurance	Financial Services	Service, team effectiveness, stakeholder engagement training	Asia, Sth America
Concorde	Oil Services	Project management, selling skills, business writing	Australia, Middle East
Affinity Resources	IT Project Management	Green Project Management— Stakeholder Management	China, India

TESTIMONIALS

"IMPACT Corporate Training delivered a training program designed to improve our stakeholder engagement skills. So far we have seen project savings of over USD 500,000. This has come about from delegates applying the influencing techniques to prevent project delays and deliver them earlier. The benefits are way beyond our expectations."

Jose Ramirez, General Manager, Affinity Resources

Attachment 3: Implementation Plan

Customer Centricity Project	PROJECT MILESTONES

ACTION	DONE BY	WHO	STATUS	COMMENTS
DATES				
Dubai Sept 2-3, London, Sept 5-6	1-Jul	Oriental		
Book training room	1-Jul	Oriental		
Arrange training aids—five flipcharts	1-Jul	Oriental		
FLIGHTS / ACCOMODATION				
Advise of suitable accommodation for trainers	1-Jul	Oriental	Done	
Book through Oriental Travel	1-Aug	IMPACT		-
PARTICIPANTS				
Confirm nominations / attendees	1-Aug	Oriental		
Arrange links to Webex and E-learning, test, send to IMPACT	1-Aug	Oriental	Done	All delegates to receive links. Oriental to test in advance
Send Joining Instruction	1-Aug	Oriental		Ensure reference to pre-work
Send pre-work: Client Opportunity Report, Case Study, E-learning Links, WebEx links	10-Aug	IMPACT		Ensure Website is completed and tested
Engage participants to welcome them and ensure they have completed and sent pre-work.	17-Aug	IMPACT		Oriental to send list of delegates
Call delegates two weeks after the training to discuss their learning outcomes and actions since the training.	21-Sep	IMPACT		Direct them to website to record their plans
GUESTS				
Identify suitable speakers and book time—advising of the venue, date and timing	1-Aug	Oriental		
Send slide deck for review	1-Aug	IMPACT		Need to update due to regulatory changes—check with Peter White at Oriental

Prepare Speakers Agenda and distribute	17-Aug	IMPACT		Unchanged from Workshop 1
Call to ensure confirmation of attendance	24-Aug	Oriental		
MATERIALS				
Ensure handout and slide materials are current and correctly branded	1-Aug	IMPACT		Double check with Oriental Marketing— Grace Fong
Liaise with product managers and guest speakers to ensure alignment of content	17-Aug	IMPACT		Prakash Kumar to coordinate internally
Send finished materials to Oriental for printing	17-Aug	IMPACT		Omar Kaiaz to coordinate and print locally
Ensure materials are printed, placed in folders and are at the venue	31-Aug	Oriental		Omar Kaiaz to coordinate and print locally
FEEDBACK SHEETS				
Collate results and submit report	21-Sep	IMPACT		

Your company Logo and website in the footer

Appendix 3. Sample Meeting Agenda

Setting an agenda indicates competence. Think about it in advance—what do you want your client to get out of the meeting? What do you want? Are they compatible objectives? There is a golden rule for meeting agendas—The Client's Agenda is Your Agenda.

Why? Well why are you having a meeting? Pushing Snake Oil Medicine, or finding out more about your client, and what they want?

Here's a BAD AGENDA

Hi John, see you mon @ 10. It will be good to catch up and shoot the breeze on the CCP. Couple of items to discuss were IMPACT's global profile and our main clients in Financial Services; significant achievements and client testimonials. We just won a major deal with Eurasio Finance, so it will be good to talk about that as well—I think you know the Treasurer, Mary ???. We should also talk about how things are going with Oriental's Customer-Centric project / proposal. Not sure where you are with that but know that we will be good value in driving it through, given the work we did with Concordia. Hopefully we can have some lunch afterwards if yourve got time. I'm bringing Cynthia as well. Remember I told you we were hiring her from Santo? She's pretty well versed in Customer Service projects. Cheers Bern

What's wrong with this agenda?

- What date is the meeting?
- Where is it?
- Who is going to be there from each team?
- What are the main points?
- What is the client's agenda?

- Who is Mary?
- Is it Oriental's Customer-Centric Project or a Proposal? Get it right
- "Not sure where you are at" implies laziness and informality. "Project update" is a lot better.
- How do we know "we will be good value in driving it through" if we don't know what "It" is?
- Lunch arrangement is too casual—are you paying for lunch or not?
- Who is Cynthia? What is her background? What is she contributing to the meeting? What has "being well versed in Customer Service" got to do with anything? Be specific.
- Cheers, Bern is too casual. Being formal doesn't hurt.

Here's a **BETTER** one

Hi John, I am confirming our meeting for Monday July 18 at 10am in your office, Level 17. Cynthia, our Customer Service Director, will join us. You met her at our Client Event in May. Cynthia's profile is attached. She has outstanding credentials in Customer Service strategy implementation.

Agenda

- Introducing Cynthia
- Oriental's agenda—please advise your most important items—John
- Oriental's Customer-Centricity project—status update—John
- How IMPACT can help at this stage—all

We expect to finish the meeting at 1200. I have booked the Outrigger Restaurant for 1215. We can walk from your office.

Please let me know if you would like to invite anyone so I can let the restaurant know.

We look forward to seeing you.

Thank you
Bern
65-9754 9451

Ring your client to make sure they received your email. Check the agenda. Formalise the meeting with an Outlook Invitation. Double check the restaurant.

NOTE: Always put your signature / phone number at the end of every email. There is nothing more frustrating that trawling through emails to find someone's phone number. Make it easy for your client.

The Client Meeting

1. Send the Agenda and get the client to confirm it: Remember—the Client's Agenda is Your Agenda.
2. Dress UP, or at least, appropriate to the client's business (Don't wear a suit on an oil rig).
3. Have business cards—don't say, "sorry, I'm just getting some new ones printed".
4. Take notes. Probe comments you don't understand.
5. Speak normally. Don't try to impress with big words.
6. Talk about your client's needs, not yours.
7. Use whiteboards an flipcharts to capture complex issues— map the process.
8. Summarise everything said.

9. Ask how you can be a better partner.
10. Tell them what you will do next.
11. Thank them for their time.
12. Follow up—send the Call Report within 24 hours.
13. Find interesting articles to send them that relate to your discussion.
14. Beforehand, check on any news affecting them—takeover, redundancies.
15. Make sure you know who is coming, and what they are interested in.
16. During introductions, check pronunciation of names.
17. Smile—but not like a Product Pushing Snake Oil Salesman.
18. Thank your client for their time. Check how much time they have, and stick to it.
19. Ask the client what they would like to discuss. Write it down. Agree the meeting agenda.
20. Lean forward to express interest—not too close.
21. Laugh at small talk, but don't overdo it—get down to business.
22. Ask about and follow the client's agenda. Ask for permission to add your own points.

Snake Oil Salesman's view

"Snake Oil Salesman—oh, sorry, I don't have any cards left, I just keep getting so many customers, I've run out"

Appendix 4: Whiteboards and flipcharts

Most people have NO IDEA how to use these indispensable sales tools. Yet they are almost as important as you are in the sales process. When you are running a sales meeting you are trying to communicate. We do this by speaking and by non-verbal means, such as writing and showing slides and diagrams. If people don't understand what you are drawing or writing on a board, you lose them. On the other hand, good clear handwriting to capture the main points or draw the current process helps everyone understand a little better. Make no mistake, being able to write and draw on flipcharts and boards is an *essential* sales skill.

Here are some tips:

1. Buy a flipchart and whiteboard and put it in your office
2. Practice writing on it. Dark blue and black are the ONLY colours to use for the main text. Red for Headings and Arrows, Green for minor details. Why? Blue and Black are easy to see, Red is hard on the eyes, and Green is almost invisible.
3. Carry blue and black whiteboard markers in your briefcase / backpack. Get the Chisel-pointed ones—they make your writing thicker and easier to read. During client meetings, ask for permission to capture details on the board. Everyone will look at the board or chart.
4. Suddenly you are out of Snake Oil Salesman mode. You're not trying to sell them anything. You're trying to understand the puzzle. It's like a jigsaw puzzle—much easier to understand when you see it laid out on the table.

5. Remember the IMPACT model. Break the conversation into stages, and logically explore the needs.
6. Write slowly, using big letters. Don't scribble in a corner. You lose the audience.
7. When the conversation concludes, use the board / chart to CONFIRM understanding. Everyone can see what happened in the meeting. We're all in this together.
8. Take a photo of the writing on your phone. Summarise it in the Call Report. Send it to the client.

Using charts and boards totally differentiates you from the competition. You will be that far in front, you'll be lonely!

ABOUT THE AUTHOR

Bernard Jones is a cancer survivor, entrepreneur, salesman, trainer, and part-time writer.

He has worked in sales and training for over 30 years and taught thousands of people around the world how to sell. His sardonic humour and self-deprecating style brings a stark reality to the world of selling: it's not easy out there, you possibly lose more deals than you win. But there are some good tools to help you. This book is one of them.

His message is straight, a simple philosophy taught to him by his father Desmond. "You're dead for a long time - go for it".

In loving memory of my great Dad, Desmond.

Please buy this book so Bern can become a full-time writer.